AFRICAN WRITERS SERIES

Founding editor   Chinua Achebe

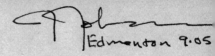

A Book of
AFRICAN VERSE

compiled and edited by

JOHN REED *and* CLIVE WAKE

HEINEMANN
LONDON IBADAN NAIROBI LUSAKA

Heinemann Educational Books Ltd
48 Charles Street, London WIX 8AH
P.M.B. 5205 Ibadan · P.O. Box 45314 Nairobi
P.O. Box 3966 Lusaka
EDINBURGH MELBOURNE AUCKLAND KINGSTON TORONTO
HONG KONG SINGAPORE KUALA LUMPUR NEW DELHI

ISBN 0 435 90008 0

First published 1964
Reprinted 1965, 1966, 1967, 1969, 1970, 1976, 1978

Printed Offset Litho and bound in Great Britain by
Cox & Wyman Ltd, London, Fakenham and Reading

CONTENTS

vii

ACKNOWLEDGEMENTS

For permission to include the poems in this anthology acknowledgement is made to the following: The Faith Press for *The Lonely Soul* by Raphael Armattoe and *Stanley meets Mutesa* by David Rubadiri; Mbari for *You may well cry*, *Night Rain*, and *Ibadan* by J. P. Clark, *For Georgette* by Christopher Okigbo and *Were I to choose* by Gabriel Okara; Éditions Seghers for translations of *Les Lignes de nos mains* and *Feuille au vent* by Bernard Dadié and *Tu marcheras en paix* by Martial Sinda; M. Léopold Sédar Senghor for translations of *Défi à la Force* by David Diop and *Chant XXII* by Jacques Rabémananjara; Les amis de Rabéarivelo for translations of *Ton Oeuvre*, *Flutistes*, *Cactus*, *Quel rat invisible*, *Lente*, and *Trois naissances du jour* by Jean-Joseph Rabéarivelo; Oxford University Press and Éditions du Seuil for translations of *Tout le long du jour*, *Taga pour Mbaye Dyob*, *Aux soldats negro-americains*, *Ndessé*, and *Le Message* by Léopold Sédar Senghor; Mr Martin Banham for *A bus ride* by U. I. Ukwu and *Superstition* and *It could have been a lonely night* by Minji Karibo; and Présence Africaine for *Greetings to all Afric's lands* by Sam Epelle, and translations of *Viatique* and *Souffle* by Birago Diop and *Les Heures*, *Vagues*, and *Afrique* by David Diop.

NOTE

Line numbers have been given to some of the poems for ease of reference.

INTRODUCTION

This book gives a selection of the poetry written by Africans in English, together with some translations into English of poems written by Africans in French. It is not an anthology drawn from the whole field of African poetry. It does not represent the traditional poetry of Africa's many vernacular languages, nor does it represent the poetry which is today growing up side by side with the traditional poetry, the work of modern African poets who write and publish their poetry instead of reciting it and who are often influenced by European poetry, but who continue to use their own vernacular languages. Whether the future of African poetry lies mainly with this vernacular poetry or whether it lies in the development of an African tradition in French poetry and English poetry we do not know. But for many years it is probable that some African poets will continue writing in the African languages, and some in the main European languages which are used in Africa for administration, education and international purposes.

The poet who chooses to write in his own vernacular can only reach those who speak his language. A Nigerian who writes in Yoruba, a Senegalese who writes in Serer, will be cut off by the language he uses from the majority of his fellow citizens in the Nigerian Federation or the Republic of Senegal. On the other hand, if he writes in English or in French, although people from all parts of his country and indeed from many parts of Africa and the rest of the world will be able to read his work, he will not be intelligible to those people even from his own village who have not learnt a European language.

A choice like this faced some poets in Europe in the Middle Ages and the sixteenth and seventeenth centuries. If they decided to write in Latin, their poetry would be understood in every country of Europe, but only by the educated. If they wrote in the vernacular language of their country, in English or French or Spanish, they would find very few readers outside their own countrymen. But among them, of course, they could appeal not only to the learned but also to those who were no more than literate in their mother tongue.

African poets have chosen to write in English or French sometimes because they feel that what they have to say can be better expressed in a language which has been developed for literary purposes for many hundreds of years; sometimes because what they have to say is for readers all over the continent of Africa and outside Africa; sometimes because they are anxious for poetic fame wider than the frontiers of their own country. Some poets have written both in a European language and in their own vernacular. James Jolobe's *Thuthula* is the poet's own English version of a poem which he composed originally in his own language, Xhosa. Jean-Joseph Rabéarivelo wrote all the poems included in this book not only in French but also in Malagasy, the language of his native Madagascar.

As already mentioned, we have included in this book, along with poems written by Africans in English, our own translations into English of poems originally by Africans in French. It happens that the best French African poets write in a free verse which it is possible to translate directly without losing too much of the poem's form. But of course a translation is never a perfect equivalent of the poem in its original language, and we have always indicated at the

2

end of the poem when the version given is a translation made by the editors.

African poetry in European languages mixes influences from Africa and from Europe. It is difficult to use a language without using some of the literary traditions which have grown up with that language, and most of the poets in this book have been influenced by the traditions of English and French poetry. Some have been influenced by a particular English or French poet and even by a particular poem. James Jolobe's *Thuthula*, for example, although it is a version of his Xhosa poem, is closely modelled on the narrative blank verse of the nineteenth-century English poet, Alfred, Lord Tennyson. Mostly the influences are more modern than this. Gabriel Okara, for example, writes in a way which suggests he has been deeply influenced by Dylan Thomas, who died in 1953. David Rubadiri's poem *Stanley meets Mutesa* has been influenced by T. S. Eliot's *The Journey of the Magi* which begins in a similar way:

> A cold coming we had of it
> Just the worst time of the year
> For a journey.

As we would expect, the African poets who write in French are influenced by French poets and the French poetic tradition. Modern French poetry has often a looser structure and a more rhetorical style than English poetry of the same period, and this difference is carried over into the African poetry written in the two languages. Poets are almost always great imitators, and much poetry in this book belongs to English and French literature as well as to the literature of Africa.

But imitation is sometimes of African and not European traditions, and there are poets who are really adapting African vernacular literature into a European language.

3

Adeboye Babalola's poetry is an example of this. Jean-Joseph Rabéarivelo was a poet who began by writing verse closely imitating the French poetry of the late nineteenth century (none of this work is included here), but who developed through his short life away from this direct French influence until his latest work, represented here by the *Two Old Merina Songs*, is closely based on the poetic dialogues or *hain-teny* in popular use once among the people of Madagascar. Flavien Ranaivo has continued this work where Rabéarivelo left it at the time of his death. A poem such as *Traditional Theme from Merina* is very close to an actual Malagasy folk-poem.

Besides drawing on African vernacular poetry, African poets also draw on Africa for subject matter, re-telling stories from African history and legend, describing African folk-beliefs and customs, and putting into poetry the appearance of African landscapes. They also try to express the political experience that Africa has been going through in the last twenty years and is still going through today. Some of this is revolutionary poetry, asserting Africa, African traditions and values against Europe. Many of the poets have spent much time in Europe and their poetry tells of the African's experience in Europe, sometimes as protest, sometimes as satire, sometimes lyrically. You will probably notice a difference in these matters between poetry written in French and that written in English. Of course not all the political battles and changes in Africa have produced poetry. Very little, for example, has come from the struggle in Southern and Central Africa. Poetry deals with politics, with the enthusiasm of building new nations and bringing about great changes as much as with the matters that are important in the poet's personal life. The most important poetry, however, is not always the poetry that has what by ordinary standards would be considered the most important

4

subjects . . . and great subjects do not always produce their great poet.

African poetry in English and French has still only a very short history. All the poetry in this book belongs to the last thirty years and much of it is written by poets who are still young. We have tried to choose the best while representing as many different kinds of poetry as possible. For some of the poems we have included high claims cannot be made. But already much of the life and feeling and thought of the continent is finding expression through the means of poetry.

Raphael Armattoe

Born in Ghana. By profession a medical doctor and an anthropologist. He worked in Ireland for ten years, and then returned to Ghana where he found himself unable to accept the political trends in the country. He was killed in Germany a few years ago in an accident.

Boyhood Dreams

They have thought as young men think
    Of love, fame and glory;
They have found as old men find
    Life's tales stale and hoary.

They had hoped as children hope,
    To pick life's pleasant gains;
And now they walk with bowed heads,
    Like drenched men from the rains.

The Lonely Soul

I met an old woman
Talking by herself
Down a lonely road.
Talking to herself,
Down a country road.
Child, you cannot know
Why folks talk alone.

If the road be long
And travellers none,
A man talks to himself.
If showers of sorrows
Fall down like arrows
The lone wayfarer
May talk by himself.
So an old woman
On lone country roads,
Laughing all the time,
May babble to herself
To keep the tears away.
Woman, you are sad!
'Tis the same with me.

George Awoonor-Williams

Born in 1935 at Keta, in the Volta region of Ghana. He studied at Achimota and the University of Ghana, Accra. He now teaches in the Institute of African Studies at the University. He is on the editorial committee of *Okyeame*, the Ghana literary review, and has contributed to *Transition*.

Rediscovery

When our tears are dry on the shore
and the fishermen carry their nets home
and the seagulls return to bird island
and the laughter of children recedes at night
there shall still linger the communion we forged
the feast of oneness whose ritual we partook of

There shall still be the eternal gateman
who will close the cemetery doors
and send the late mourners away
It cannot be the music we heard that night
that still lingers in the chambers of memory
It is the new chorus of our forgotten comrades
and the halleluyahs of our second selves

Adeboye Babalola

Yoruba poet from Nigeria. Graduate of Cambridge University.
He was a schoolmaster for some years, and now teaches in the
Institute of African Studies of the University of Ife. He is
known for his renderings into English verse of Yoruba folk
tales.

A Tale of the Maize Plant

I don't know at all, but I wish I knew
What clothes the Maize Plant wore when first he came
To this Origbo area from Olufe Town.
But I know for sure that he was disguised
As he journeyed here, and when he reached Moro
The nearest settlement in Origbo,
He asked the people of the place whether or not
The Water-god was living there among them.
And they replied, 'Oh no, he is not here,'
Therefore the Maize Plant ordered them to find   10
And have in readiness for him, when next
He visited Moro, two *olugbere* rats,
Two fishes of the *olugbala* breed,
And two large pods of ripened kola-nuts.

9

Then the Maize Plant travelled on from Moro,
And soon he reached that village, Yakoyo,
So called because its first inhabitants
Erected many stalls along the road,
And there invited passing travellers
To come and buy good food as well as drinks   20
On which they might feed full and be refreshed.
(But, alas, when journeying men call there these days,
They find the fare so very costly that
They cannot refresh themselves quite well
Without incurring debt and starving soon.)
At this Yakoyo also, the Maize Plant
Asked the people, 'Is the god of water here?'
And they too said that the god was not there.
So he enjoined them thus: 'By the time I return
Have ready for me two *olugbere* rats,   30
Two fishes of the *olugbala* kind,
And two large pods of wholesome kola-nuts.'

Next the Maize Plant reached Ipetumodu,
That Origbo town whose appositional name,
Is Moriasala, due to its being,
Initially, a home for refugees,
Yorubas who fled from Oyo town when it was sacked
By Fulanis seven score years ago.
To the people here he made the same request
Regarding if the Water-god was there.   40
When they replied, 'Oh no, he is not here,'
To them the Maize Plant gave the same advice,
And then he journeyed on to Asipa,
The next village in Origbo, also called
Elenpe, meaning 'Small-and-beautiful'.

10

'Is the god of water here?' he inquired.
The people answered that the Water-god
Was not among the gods they worshipped there.
Therefore the Maize Plant ordered them to find
And have in readiness for him when next   50
He visited their town, two *olugbere* rats,
Two fishes of the *olugbala* breed,
And two large pods of ripened kola-nuts.
Then, quitting Asipa, the Maize Plant left
Origbo, and went to Gbongan,
A town with many attributive names;
Gbongan, Akinfemwa, Oleojogunesin.
B'o-jogun-erin-a-gba-a-l''o-re—
Gbongan founded by Akinfemwa,
Whose motto was: 'Never is a horse   60
Gained in legacy by an idle man.'

   Disappointed by the reply he got
To his question from the Gbongan people,
The Maize Plant advised them as the Origbos,
And quickly made for Ikire,
A town whose dwellers are proud to be called
Omo Ewu Ojele, Ewu-fi-'le-han-mi-
F'ona-han-mi; Ewu-o-je f'abuja-'le 'Kire-
Han-'mo Ogidan, which means 'Descendants
Of Mr Ewu Ojele, Ewu,   70
Who gladly takes visitors round his town,
Showing them all the houses and the streets,
But never pointing out to them by-passes
And short-cuts leading to and from the town.'

   'Is the god of water here?' the Maize Plant
Asked these Ile 'Kire inhabitants.

11

And they delighted him tremendously,
By saying, 'Oh yes, the Water-god *is* here,'
And showing him the many little shrines
In which they worshipped that god in their town.   80
   So the Maize Plant disclosed his identity
To the Ikires, and he dwelt with them.
Thus the Maize Plant became a citizen
Of Ikire, Omo Ewu Ojele.

   It was not I who made this pleasant song,
It was my bosom friend, Odejinmi,
Elerineye Omo' le Jagun,
Odejinmi, a very humorous man,
Easily amused and dignified in laughter,
Belonging to the compound of our chief, Jagun.   90

The Trouble-Lover

Ojo is his name, Ojo the Trouble-Lover.
He loudly calls to Trouble when it's passing by,
Inviting him to come into his home and spend some
   time.
With his *arugogo*, a hook-tipped pole,
He hooks Disquiet's feet and makes it halt perforce,
That he may have the pleasure of its company.
When he finds in his way a tangled coil
Of Trouble Rope, he knowingly puts a foot in it
And gladly drags it on with him.
He invites a good-for-nothing person to his house,   10
Just for love of quarrelling.
He's a reckless rascal through and through;

He hardly hesitates before he knifes
A person who does not agree with him,
And when'er he hears a quarrel going on,
Or sees some people hard exchanging blows,
He tries to find out what has caused the ire—
Whatever lies at the bottom of the case.
He's as frightful as the Iron god, for
He sometimes runs about in the streets   20
Holding high aggressively a glittering axe.

If a boy is mischievous and his mother likes this fact,
We owe the neighbours sympathetic greetings oft,
For the trouble which the boy daily puts them in.
True to type among the mischiefs of the Trouble-
    Lover's doing
Are these: 'I will marry that girl,' he says,
'I will marry her unfailingly,
No matter to whom she has already been betrothed.'
He is fond of marrying wives of other men,
And so he often finds himself in hell at home.   30
For sometimes his stolen wives are past-mistresses
In the art of domineering over husbands, of all kinds.
For instance, he once married Shango's wife,
That is, the God of Thunder's spouse,
But in his house she made him ill at ease
By belching fire from her mouth whene'er she spoke.

He often proves as obstinate as Mortar was
When fussily he ran to the Mortar-Pounding Square,
In the town of Yampounding-Speciality,
And said, 'I will become the Oba here,   40
I will ascend the throne, no matter who objects.'

His bosom friends tried hard to make him change his
    mind.
'No! No! Don't force your way to gain the Obaship!'
Again, Mortar stubbornly refused the advice,
He still insisted on becoming king.
At length, indeed, he did ascend the throne.
Then he regrettingly experienced that hard fact
That 'Uneasy lies the head that wears the crown.'
Mortar can never have rest and peace of mind,
Because of several of the laws in vogue among the
    people there: 50
'In Mortar's absence, no-one shall pound any yam,
In Mortar's absence, no woman shall pound her
    grains of maize.
In Mortar's absence, no-one shall make yam flour,
In Mortar's absence, no powerful, pounded medicine
    shall be made.'
Calls for Mortar's services were numberless,
And he suffered diverse agonies in consequence.
Red pepper berries stung his eyes,
They also stung his mouth and nose,
And made him feel uncomfortably hot
Within his stomach's walls.   60
His ears were split, a hole was bored through his chest,
And, at last, his entire frame was split in two.

It's the Trouble-Lover who carried home from farm
A dead bush-fowl, despite his knowing very well
That it's a widely held belief among his class
That this act will make evil spirits kill
His mother, or compel his father to ascend
The Elders' Hill.

And finally, it's the Trouble-Lover who tells you,
'I want to sit with you.'   70
If you reply, 'There is no room,'
He will retort, 'Sure, there's room for me to sit
On the summit of your nose.'
Such is the Trouble-Lover;
For him, there is no rest, day or night.

Kwesi Brew

Born in 1928 at Cape Coast, Ghana. He studied at the University
College, now the University of Ghana, Accra. He entered the
Public Service in 1953 and at present works in the Foreign
Office in Accra.

Ancestral Faces

They sneaked into the limbo of time.
But could not muffle the gay jingling
Bells on the frothy necks
Of the sacrificial sheep that limped and nodded after them;
They could not hide the moss on the bald pate
Of their reverent heads;
And the gnarled barks of the *wawa* trees;
Nor the rust on the ancient state-swords;
Nor the skulls studded with grinning cowries;
They could not silence the drums,
The fibre of their souls and ours—
The drums that whisper to us behind black sinewy hands.
They gazed,
And sweeping like white locusts through the forests
Saw the same men, slightly wizened,

Shuffle their sandalled feet to the same rhythms,
They heard the same words of wisdom uttered
Between puffs of pale blue smoke:
They saw us,
And said: They have not changed!

John Pepper Clark

Nigerian poet and playwright, born in 1935 in the Ijaw country
of the Niger Delta. Studied at University College, now the
University of Ibadan, where he founded the poetry magazine called
The Horn. He has worked as a journalist and recently went to
Princeton University in the United States. His play, *The Song of a
Goat*, was performed and published in Ibadan by the Mbari
Writers' Club in 1962. Mbari has also published a volume of his
poems.

You may well cry . . .

You may well cry. But this is nothing
To beat your breast. It was how
We all began and will end. A child,
Once out of the womb, will shout,
Even like the chick or seedling
Out of its shell. And whether
For pain, for laugh, who can tell? But now you
Have lived to this day, perhaps you are ripe
To hazard a crack at life's nut. Still,
Do not, my people, venture overmuch
Else in unravelling the knot, you
Entangle yourselves. It is enough
You know now that each day we live
Hints at why we cried out at birth.

Night Rain

What time of night it is
I do not know
Except that like some fish
Doped out of the deep
I have bobbed up bellywise
From stream of sleep
And no cocks crow.
It is drumming hard here
And I suppose everywhere
Droning with insistent ardour upon   10
Our roof thatch and shed
And thro' sheaves slit open
To lightning and rafters
I can not quite make out overhead
Great water drops are dribbling
Falling like orange or mango
Fruits showered forth in the wind
Or perhaps I should say so
Much like beads I could in prayer tell
Them on string as they break   20
In wooden bowls and earthenware
Mother is busy now deploying
About our roomlet and floor.
Although it is so dark
I know her practised step as
She moves her bins, bags and vats
Out of the run of water
That like ants filing out of the wood
Will scatter and gain possession
Of the floor. Do not tremble then   30

But turn, brothers, turn upon your side
Of the loosening mats
To where the others lie.
We have drunk tonight of a spell
Deeper than the owl's or bat's
That wet of wings may not fly.
Bedraggled up on the iroko, they stand
Emptied of hearts, and
Therefore will not stir, no, not
Even at dawn for then   40
They must scurry in to hide.
So let us roll over on our back
And again roll to the beat
Of drumming all over the land
And under its ample soothing hand
Joined to that of the sea
We will settle to sleep of the innocent and free.

Ibadan

Ibadan,
      running splash of rust
and gold—flung and scattered
among seven hills like broken
china in the sun.

S. D. Cudjoe

Born in 1910, at Lomé, Togo. Studied medicine in Edinburgh and Glasgow from 1932–39 and for many years practised in South London. Returned to Ghana in 1955. He is an authority on African music.

Reincarnation

They came by sea,
Innumerable like the surfs they came,
Dressed in sea-green robes
And cloaks of frothy white lace.
They came and went, and yet more came,
By night they came
On their fateful journey nowhere,
Weaving eternal patterns on the golden sand.

By land they came, the living dead,
To tidal threshold of new life.
I heard mysterious voices
Beyond my mother's heaving breath,
Beyond the wind's gentle tread
On the depth of night.
Until at cockrow, Nature sang,
And Dawn beckoned me enchantingly
With dew bejewelled hands.

Bernard B. Dadié

Born in 1916 near Abidjan, Ivory Coast. Educated in Dakar and for some years worked there for the Institut Français d'Afrique Noire. Now in the government service in the Ivory Coast. He has published a number of prose works and two volumes of poetry: *Afrique debout* (poèmes) (1950); *Légendes Africaines* (1953); *Le Pagne noir* (1955); *La Ronde des Jours* (poèmes) (1956); *Climbié* (1956); *Un nègre à Paris* (1959).

The Lines of our Hands

The lines of our hands
Are not parallel lines
Nor roads through the mountains
Nor fissures on tree trunks
Nor the scars of homeric fights.

The lines of our hands
Are not longitude lines

Nor furrows in the plains
Nor partings in the hair
Nor paths through the bush

No they are not
   gutters for grief
   channels for tears
   drainage for hate
   ropes for the hanged

nor portions
nor parts
nor pieces
  of this . . . and that . . .

The lines of our hands
  not Yellow
  Black
  White
No they are not frontiers
Ditches between our villages
Cords to bind faggots of bitterness

The lines of our hands
Are the lines of Life,
  of Fate,
  of Heart,
  of Love.

Gentle bonds
To bind us
To one another
The living to the dead.

The lines of our hands
  not white
  not black
  not yellow

The lines of our hands
Bind the nosegays of our dreams.

Translated from the French

Leaf in the Wind

I am the man the colour of Night
Leaf in the wind, I go at the drift of my dreams.

I am the tree putting forth shoots in spring
The dew that hums in the baobab's hollow.

Leaf in the wind, I go at the drift of my dreams.

I am the man they complain of
Because opposed to formality
The man they laugh at
Because opposed to barriers.

Leaf in the wind, I go at the drift of my dreams.

I am the man they talk about:
    'Oh him!'
Him you cannot hold
The breeze that touches you and is gone

Leaf in the wind, I go at the drift of my dreams.

Captain at the stern
Scanning the scudding clouds
For the earth's powerful eye;
Ship without sail
That glides on the sea

Leaf in the wind, I go at the drift of my dreams.

I am the man whose dreams
Are manifold as the stars

More murmurous than swarms of bees
More smiling than children's smiles
More sonorous than echoes in the woods.

Leaf in the wind, I go at the drift of my dreams.

Translated from the French

Birago Diop

Born in 1906 in Dakar, Senegal. A veterinary surgeon by profession. He has been Senegalese Ambassador to Tunisia since 1960. He has published one volume of poetry, *Leurres et Lueurs* (1960), but he is best known for his two collections of folk-tales: *Les Contes d'Amadou Koumba* (1947) and *Les Nouveaux contes d'Amadou Koumba* (1958). Recently he has published a third volume entitled *Contes et Lavanes* (1963).

Viaticum

In one of the three vessels
The three vessels where certain evenings come
The souls serene and satisfied,
The breathings of the ancestors,
Ancestors who once were men
Forefathers who once were sages
My mother dipped three fingers,
Three fingers of her left hand:
Thumb and index and second finger;
And I myself dipped three fingers:
Three fingers of the right hand:
Thumb and index and second finger.

With three fingers red in the blood,
Blood of dog,
Blood of bull,
Blood of goat,
My mother three times touched me.
She touched my forehead with her thumb,
With her index my left breast
And with her second finger touched my navel,
I myself held out my fingers red in the blood
Blood of dog,
Blood of bull
Blood of goat,
I held out my three fingers to the winds
To the winds from the North, to the winds from the East
To the winds of the South, to the winds from the Sunset;
And I raised my three fingers to the Moon,
To the full Moon, the Moon naked and full
At the bottom of the largest vessel.

When I had plunged my fingers into the sand
Into the sand which had grown cold
Then my Mother said: 'Go, go through the World
All your life they will follow your steps.'

And now I go
I go down the paths
Down the paths and the roads,
Beyond the sea and further, and further still
Beyond the sea and beyond what is beyond
And when I come near to the wicked,
To the men with black hearts
When I come near to the envious

To the men with black hearts
The Breathings of my Forefathers go before me.

Translated from the French

Breath

Listen more to things
Than to words that are said.
The water's voice sings
And the flame cries
And the wind that brings
The woods to sighs
Is the breathing of the dead.

Those who are dead have never gone away.
They are in the shadows darkening around,
They are in the shadows fading into day,   10
The dead are not under the ground.
They are in the trees that quiver,
They are in the woods that weep,
They are in the waters of the rivers,
They are in the waters that sleep.
They are in the crowds, they are in the homestead.
The dead are never dead.

Listen more to things
Than to words that are said.
The water's voice sings   20
And the flame cries
And the wind that brings
The woods to sighs

Is the breathing of the dead.
Who have not gone away
Who are not under the ground
Who are never dead.

Those who are dead have never gone away.
They are at the breast of the wife.
They are in the child's cry of dismay   30
And the firebrand bursting into life.
The dead are not under the ground.
They are in the fire that burns low
They are in the grass with tears to shed,
In the rock where whining winds blow
They are in the forest, they are in the homestead.
The dead are never dead.

Listen more to things
Than to words that are said.
The water's voice sings   40
And the flame cries
And the wind that brings
The woods to sighs
Is the breathing of the dead.

And repeats each day
The Covenant where it is said
That our fate is bound to the law,
And the fate of the dead who are not dead
To the spirits of breath who are stronger than they.
We are bound to Life by this harsh law   50
And by this Covenant we are bound
To the deeds of the breathings that die
Along the bed and the banks of the river,

To the deeds of the breaths that quiver
In the rock that whines and the grasses that cry
To the deeds of the breathings that lie
In the shadow that lightens and grows deep
In the tree that shudders, in the woods that weep,
In the waters that flow and the waters that sleep,
To the spirits of breath which are stronger than they 60
That have taken the breath of the deathless dead
Of the dead who have never gone away
Of the dead who are not now under the ground.

     Listen more to things
     Than to words that are said.
     The water's voice sings
     And the flame cries
     And the wind that brings
     The woods to sighs
     Is the breathing of the dead.   70

Translated from the French

David Diop

Born in Bordeaux, France, in 1927, of a Senegalese father and a Cameroonian mother. Published a small volume of verse, *Coups de Pilon* (1956) which showed great promise. He was killed in an air crash in 1960.

Waves

    The wild breakers of freedom
    Lash, lash the maddened Beast
    From yesterday's slave springs a soldier

The Suez docker, the Hanoï coolie
All those poisoned with fatal creeds
Fling their huge song into the breakers
The wild breakers of freedom
Lashing, lashing the maddened Beast.

Translated from the French

Defiance against Force

You, bowing, you, crying
You, dying, like that, one day without knowing why.
You, struggling, you watching over another's rest
You, looking no longer with laughter in your eyes
You, my brother, your face full of fear and suffering
    Stand up and shout NO!

Translated from the French

Times

There are times for dreaming
In the calm of nights by the hollow of silence
There are times for doubting
And the heavy veil of words is torn with sighs
There are times for suffering
Along the roads of war under our mothers' eyes
There are times for loving
In the huts of light where the unique flesh sings
There is what colours the days to come
As the sun colours the flesh of plants
And in times of madness

In times of impatience
There is always the most fruitful seed
Of the times that bring the poised and certain stance.

Translated from the French

Africa

Africa my Africa
Africa of proud warriors in the ancestral savannahs
Africa my grandmother sings of
Beside her distant river
I have never seen you
But my gaze is full of your blood
Your black blood spilt over the fields
The blood of your sweat
The sweat of your toil
The toil of slavery
The slavery of your children
Africa, tell me Africa,
Are you the back that bends
Lies down under the weight of humbleness?
The trembling back striped red
That says yes to the sjambok on the roads of noon?
Solemnly a voice answers me
'Impetuous child, that young and sturdy tree
That tree that grows
There splendidly alone among white and faded flowers
Is Africa, your Africa. It puts forth new shoots
With patience and stubbornness puts forth new shoots
Slowly its fruits grow to have
The bitter taste of liberty.'

Translated from the French

Sam Epelle

Born in Ibadan, Nigeria. The poem included here was originally published in the review, *Présence Africaine*. He is the author of *The Promise of Nigeria* and is now working with the Nigerian Railway Corporation.

Greetings to all Afric's Lands

EAST, NORTH, SOUTH, WEST

Greetings to lands of yams and palms;
Greetings to lands of cocoa and groundnuts;
Greetings to lands of gold
Greetings to lands of plenty, maize and bananas and oranges
Greetings to lands of coffee and rice;
Greetings to Sahara, Kalahari, Nile, Niger, Congo, Zambesi
    and all;
Greetings to mangrove swamps, sandy shores, forests;
Greetings to huts and houses, cities and villages;
Greetings to the leopard, monkey, elephant, hippo, ostrich,
    vulture, chimpanzee, crocodile;
Greetings, kind and true, to other beasts and other birds.
Afric's lands are full of men of power and tomorrow;
There are lands of good, brave men with souls their own,
Lands of strong men with heads raised high;
They are great lands—Afric's lands of the matchet.
The farm in the forest, the matchet that clears the bush;
The farmer's hut, the yams stacked high in the barn ready
    for the market;
The leaves of the cocoyam spreading to welcome the harvest
    that must ruin them;

The twitting of the sparrow; the hoot of the owl; the cooing
　　of the pigeon;
The twig that breaks under the foot and you look around;
　　there is no cause for alarm; you go forward;
Farmland spreads hither and thither; yam tendrils coil round
　　tall bamboo poles;
Banana and rubber plantations spread far and wide—there
　　is no end to the cavalcade.
The cutting of the palm fruit; the tapping of the
　　rubber;
The struggle of men who sought to end the slave trade and
　　bring peace to Afric's lands;
Freetown, Liberia, Wilberforce, Livingstone, the Slave
　　Coast, Zanzibar and Liberty;
The fight, the victory, the death, to lighten darkness;
The memories of bygone days; the hopes of the future;
The momentary joy of hope gladdens the hearts of men in
　　Afric's lands;
The joy of actions taken by themselves, of homes which
　　they can call their own.
Matchet, Cham!
The thick forest, before its onslaught,
Trees and shrubs tumble down all flat;
A big fire razes all to ashes.
Matchet, Zam!
The sapling falls, the ground is cleared;
Houses rise, with raffia roofs and muddy walls;
Or the farm hoed out with care and toil
Is ready for the planting—yams and cassava; greens and
　　pumpkins;
And so from day to day the matchet rises, falls,
And Time moves on in Afric's lands.

Joseph Gatuiria

Born in Kenya. Studied at Makerere College, Kampala, in Uganda, and contributed to the English Department literary paper, *Pen-Point*, from which this poem is taken.

Kariuki

The hour of midnight met with a gathering of mothers,
Their only talk—names upon names.
  'It will be my nephew' one said,
  'No, my sister's cousin'. 'Kirahiu
  Is the name or should it be Mwangi?'

Then I heard the delicate squeal of a baby
  (It is of an hour's age)
Caused no less than a whole village to awake.
  What causes them to awake?
  And an old man comes struggling into the house.

'How are you, Kariuki?' This he whispers
To the deaf stranger of this world.
  Whereupon the 'Kariuki' begins its endless journey.
  It floats from mouth to mouth
  'It's a boy?' 'Kariuki is born!'
  The old warrior is born again.

Aig Higo

Born in Nigeria. Studied at University College, Ibadan, and then at Leeds University. The poem included here is taken from the Leeds University poetry magazine, *Poetry and Audience*. Has recently published poems in the literary review *Transition* (Kampala). He now teaches English at St. Andrew's College, Oyo, in Western Nigeria.

Bird's Eye-View

I
    took a maiden flight over winter into England
    chirping loud the lyrics of youth, the sun-bathing palms—
    my wings are clipped, perched square on a tree,
    handed darkness early at intervals of light
    met rebuff of fogs.

Me
    drifting with the sky into the sky
    bare-faced, self-faced to itching twigs spoke
    and listening, heard myself in the gloom.

I pecked at the palisades of doom, in vain
    that first London dawn.

Minji Karibo

Nigerian. She studied at University College, Ibadan. The poem included in this volume was originally published in *Nigerian Student Verse* 1959. She is now working at the Regional Central Library in Enugu.

Superstition

I know
    that when a grumbling old woman
Is the first thing I meet in the morning
    I must rush back to bed
    And cover my head.
That wandering sheep on a sultry afternoon
Are really men come from their dark graves
    To walk in light
    In mortal sight.
That when my left hand or eyelid twitches
Or when an owl hoots from a nearby tree
    I should need pluck
    It means bad luck
That drink spilled goes to ancestral spirits,
That witches dance in clumps of bananas;
That crumbs must be left in pots and plates
    Until the morn
    For babes unborn.
That it's wrong to stand in doorways at dusk
For the ghosts must pass—they have right of way!

That when a hidden root trips me over
  Fault's not in my foot.
  It's an evil root.
That if I sleep with feet towards the door
  I'll not long be fit
  I know it—Yes I know it!

It could have been a lonely night

It could have been a lonely night,
But tree and shade shared a common greenness;

It could have been a tearful night,
But the teasing shadows shook with laughter:

It could have been a poor night,
But the moon showered a million sequins:

It could have been a fearful night,
But the gentle breeze sang of safety:

It could have been a troubled night,
But the unruffled waters spoke of peace.

Albert Kayper Mensah

Born in 1923 at Sekondi, Ghana. Studied at Achimota College and at Cambridge and London Universities. He taught for some years at Wesley College, Kumasi, and is now Education Attaché with the Ghana Embassy in Bonn. He is the author of several plays, some of which have been broadcast in Ghana, and a large number of poems. In 1956 he won the Margaret Wrong Prize for literature.

A Second Birthday

I strolled along the Garfield avenue,
Past Knight, and the black abandoned pit latrine,
To where, way back, a bathroom could be seen,
But now, a barn house garage stands, all new.
Behind me was the road to Damascus;
Before, the College blocks, and a water-tower:
And as I walked, I saw a Lazarus
Emerge from a tomb, his death-clothes o'er his shoulder.
His powerful body freed from bandages,
A rising flame of life, from the night of death.
Uncertain yet how long the ravages,
The germs, and the million killing ways of earth
Will spare his new-found Life, his radiant grace.
And as he walked past me, I saw my face.

The Ghosts

Listen . . . it is evening in Kumasi
And the lengthening sunlight fingers stroke the town
In a final caress, and move away westward,

Drawing a blind across the sky
Behind them as they move.
Can you hear the dark blind moving?
Listen!
Listen to the groaning noises,
Wild, nightmarish, fiendish wails . . .
Voices of dreaming town   10
Dreaming now at nine o'clock.
At Kejetsia . . . the city's centre,
Bright new lights are on:
But here, where I stand,
In this deserted corner,
The lights are fading in our hearts,
And lovers have to part at sundown
If they want to meet tomorrow;
So let me go to Kejetsia
To get a taxi home.   20
Cars will cross at Kejetsia
If they dare not come near here.

They won't, or dare not come near here,
Because, from where you are,
You can hear
The offensive-defensive singing of a gang
And the clang and yell of slogans,
To keep their spirits up,
Or frighten attackers off.

Listen!   30
Did you hear it too?
The wailing of the pregnant woman
Caught under a crumbling wall blown up?
The children, terrified, and running away to safety

37

And the heavy clatter of the boots
Of a pair of racing police men?

Did you count the explosions too?
Five, I think, in a rumbling sequence,
The last, the loudest of them all . . .
And five more homes will bleed!   40
I must run to Kejetsia,
To the mocking brightness at the centre
Of the pregnant town in labour,
To get a taxi home.

Kejetsia was bare and quiet
Except for a lone figure . . . waiting . . .
Looking for a taxi home.
He moved away as I approached,
And would not speak to me.
His outstretched hand was thin and black,   50
And fluttered in the wind.
A passing taxi picked him up,
And picked me up too.
Then a curious pleasure flushed his face
To see me by his side.
We sat in silence for a while,
Then the driver spoke:
'I'll drop you, massa, at your gate,
And then . . .' 'Thank you,' I said.
'How long have you been in the town?'   60
My car companion asked.
'Six years' I said, 'a long time.'
And he, 'Enough to know the joys
Of the town in days of peace and plenty.'
This, the driver did agree with;

(And I mourned that the town was ruined.
Ruined perhaps for ever).

Suddenly,
I seemed before an aged councillor.
For the weak old man   70
In a firm, wise voice
Spoke with courage and the passion of a youth
In love with life
And said:
'Do you think that all is lost
Because your wailings reach high heaven
And your tidy, new-built mansions
Blown to bits over night?
This is not a time for tears,
For mental failure or despair   80
Though opinion now is backed
By force that often knows no meaning
And any day,
Or so it seems,
Darkening clouds may break in blood
To flood the groaning city.
But this you can PREVENT and MUST!
By learning now to LOVE each other!

This is not a time for jesting,
But for living as they did,   90
When our forbears had to save
The very ethos of the race.
These are the days when men must speak.
Shout the meaning of their souls
To the stone, the stool, the tree,
To the earth, the wall, and sky,

39

And the sun, when it appears,
But above all—to Twedeampong
Pointing to the blood of Abel
On the naked cement pavement!
You must speak to the heart that poured it.
And the evil hand that drew it.'

Suddenly there was a silence,
And I wondered where I was;
But it did not last for long,
For his voice rang out again.

'Listen . . . you whose youth is strong,
Human ways delay and sway,
Till they take a stable form
Like a lake on a bed of clay,
Supporting life, and giving beauty.
What you suffer in your day,
Is the price you have to pay
As you try to come to rest
From the swaying force of change.

You must learn what life can teach you:
And remember this, my son . . .
We have ruled ourselves before,
Though in a much more simple world.
And if your heart is sound and strong,
You may triumph where we faltered
And avoid the mocking pity
Of the man who, in his heart,
Curses and despises you.

You deserve self-government now,
But you must avoid its dangers.'

At this stage, he pulled me to him,
And in a whisper, said to me:

'If you want to make it work,
Do not fall a prey to daily   130
Fear of death, and sudden death.
Try, amid the blood and passion,
To discern a fitting answer
To the cry:
     "Self-governing what?
     Self-governing whom?"
And when an answer has been found,
With an inspiring present,
Worthy of your past and future,
And the genius of your blood,   140
You must leave the shifting sands
Of self-seeking and deceit
And erect far mightier mansions
On the rock of healthy souls.
Then . . . and only then, my son,
Will you sleep in peace at night fall,
And the lovers will be gay,
For the lights at the heart of the city
Will illumine every heart
And destroy all enmity.'   150

We had reached the College gate
But the driver would not take
The fare I had to pay him.
Instead, I saw his face transfigured
As he smiled to my companion
Sitting in the taxi.

A chilly feeling made me shiver
Then as if I knew it all,
My companion said to me . . .
'He was once my private driver   160
When we shared your world.
He and I, and countless others
Look to you to save the day . . .
Some of what we left must die
But love and keep alive the best
And let that common love
Make you Friends.'

While he spoke, the taxi left;
And as I stood and shook with fear,
I saw two black and ghostly hands   170
Fluttering in the wind.

Abioseh Nicol

Born in Sierra Leone and educated in Nigeria and Sierra Leone.
He later studied at British universities. He was awarded the
Margaret Wrong Prize and Medal for Literature in Africa in
1952. His short stories, articles and poems have appeared in
numerous English and American publications.

The Meaning of Africa

Africa, you were once just a name to me
But now you lie before me with sombre green challenge
To that loud faith for freedom (life more abundant)
Which we once professed shouting

Into the silent listening microphone
Or on an alien platform to a sea
Of white perplexed faces troubled
With secret Imperial guilt; shouting
Of you with a vision euphemistic
As you always appear   10
To your lonely sons on distant shores.

Then the cold sky and continent would disappear
In a grey mental mist.
And in its stead the hibiscus blooms in shameless scarlet
   and the bougainvillea in mauve passion
   entwines itself around strong branches
   the palm trees stand like tall proud moral women
   shaking their plaited locks against the
   cool suggestive evening breeze;
   the short twilight passes;   20
   the white full moon turns its round gladness
   towards the swept open space
   between the trees; there will be
   dancing tonight; and in my brimming heart
   plenty of love and laughter.
   Oh, I got tired of the cold northern sun
   Of white anxious ghost-like faces
   Of crouching over heatless fires
   In my lonely bedroom.
   The only thing I never tired of   30
   was the persistent kindness
   Of you too few unafraid
   Of my grave dusky strangeness.

So I came back
Sailing down the Guinea Coast.

Loving the sophistication
Of your brave new cities:
Dakar, Accra, Cotonou,
Lagos, Bathurst and Bissau;
Liberia, Freetown, Libreville,   40
Freedom is really in the mind.

Go up-country, so they said,
To see the real Africa.
For whomsoever you may be,
That is where you come from.
Go for bush, inside the bush,
You will find your hidden heart,
Your mute ancestral spirit.
And so I went, dancing on my way.

Now you lie before me passive   50
With your unanswering green challenge.
Is this all you are?
This long uneven red road, this occasional succession
Of huddled heaps of four mud walls
And thatched, falling grass roofs
Sometimes ennobled by a thin layer
Of white plaster, and covered with thin
Slanting corrugated zinc.
These patient faces on weather-beaten bodies
Bowing under heavy market loads.   60
The pedalling cyclist wavers by
On the wrong side of the road,
As if uncertain of his new emancipation.
The squawking chickens, the pregnant she-goats
Lumber awkwardly with fear across the road,

Across the windscreen view of my four-cylinder kit car.
An overladen lorry speeds madly towards me
Full of produce, passengers, with driver leaning
Out into the swirling dust to pilot his
Swinging obsessed vehicle along.   70
Beside him on the raised seat his first-class
Passenger, clutching and timid; but he drives on
At so, so many miles per hour, peering out with
Bloodshot eyes, unshaved face and dedicated look;
His motto painted on each side: Sunshine Transport,
We get you there quick, quick. The Lord is my Shepherd.

The red dust settles down on the green leaves.

I know you will not make me want, Lord,
Though I have reddened your green pastures
It is only because I have wanted so much   80
That I have always been found wanting.
From South and East, and from my West
(The sandy desert holds the North)
We look across a vast continent
And blindly call it ours.
You are not a country, Africa,
You are a concept,
Fashioned in our minds, each to each,
To hide our separate fears,
To dream our separate dreams.   90
Only those within you who know
Their circumscribed plot,
And till it well with steady plough
Can from that harvest then look up
To the vast blue inside

Of the enamelled bowl of sky
Which covers you and say
'This is my Africa' meaning
'I am content and happy.
I am fulfilled, within,
Without and roundabout
I have gained the little longings
Of my hands, my loins, my heart
And the soul that follows in my shadow.'
I know now that is what you are, Africa:
Happiness, contentment, and fulfilment,
And a small bird singing on a mango tree.

Gabriel Okara

Born in 1921 in the Ijaw district of the Niger Delta, Nigeria.
Trained as a book-binder. He now works in Enugu for the
Information Service of Eastern Nigeria.

Were I to Choose

When Adam broke the stone
and red streams raged down to
gather in the womb,
an angel calmed the storm;

And I, the breath mewed
in Cain, unblinking gaze
at the world without
from the brink of an age

That draws from the groping lips
a breast-muted cry
to thread the years.
(O were I to choose)

And now the close of one
and thirty turns, the world
of bones in Babel, and
the different tongues within
are flames the head
continually burning.

And O of this dark halo
were the third head free.

And when the harmattan
of days has parched the throat
and skin, and sucked the fever
of the head away,

Then the massive dark
descends, and flesh and bone
are razed. And (O were I
to choose) I'd cheat the worms
and silence seek in stone.

Christopher Okigbo

Born in 1932 near Onitsha, Eastern Nigeria. Studied Classics at the University College, Ibadan. He was Private Secretary to the Federal Minister of Research and Information for a short while and then a member of the library staff of the University of Nigeria, Nsukka (Eastern Nigeria). He is now Manager in West Africa for Cambridge University Press. A volume of verse, *Heavensgate*, was published in 1962 by Mbari and *The Limits* (poems) will be published shortly.

For Georgette

In the chill breath
      of the day's waking

comes the newcomer

when the draper of May
has sold out fine green
garments, and the hillsides
have made up their faces,
and the gardens,
  on their faces
a painted smile:

such synthetic welcome

at the cock's third siren
when from behind bulrushes
  waking
in the teeth of the chill Maymorn
comes the newcomer.

48

Pius Oleghe

Nigerian. Studied at University College, Ibadan, and now teaches English at Edo College, Benin. This poem is taken from *Nigerian Student Verse* 1959.

A Sudden Storm

The wind howls, the trees sway,
The loose house-top sheets clatter and clang,
The open window shuts with a bang,
And the sky makes night of day.

Helter-skelter the parents run,
Pressed with a thousand minor cares:
'Hey, you there! pack the house-wares!
And where on earth's my son?'

Home skip the little children:
'Where have you been, you naughty boy?'—
The child can feel nothing but joy,
For he loves the approach of rain.

The streets clear, the houses fill,
The noise gathers as children shout
To rival the raging wind without,
And nought that can move is still—

A bright flash!—a lighted plain;
Then, from the once-blue heavens,
Accompanied by noise that deafens,
Steadily pours the rain.

Frank Parkes

Born in Ghana 1932. He was educated in Freetown and Accra, and has been successively a university student, newspaper reporter and editor and broadcaster.

Apocalypse

In the last days,
Strange sights shall visit the earth.
Sights that may turn to blood the moon,
This sun to midnight—in the last days.

But now, when swords are not yet ploughshares,
And spears still spears
Hearken you, my little ones.

If walking, shaded by the mango tree,
Or running naked, scorched by this blazing sun,
You aught perceive   10
Now, while the arrow remains arrow,
And the miracle of spears and pruning hooks
Still remains an unseen miracle
Remember, my little ones
If perchance your infant feet do slide,
And you find yourselves in some mysterious dungeon
Of black vengeful Sasabonsam,
In realms where dogs make speech,
And horns adorn the human front;
Where mermaids in their skirts of silvery scales   20
And chattering seabeasts flout mankind—
If in this strange sub-human realm

Your eyes fall on a stone, a hard black stone,
Lifeless and muddy, that has grown a beard,
Pray children, pass silently by.
Ask no questions.
For you are face to face with the first days
And the beginning and the end are one.

And in the end shall strange sights visit earth,
Stones shall be turned to men   30
And men to stones.
Sparrows beget eagles
And sand become good grain.

So children,
If perchance you see a hare that roars
Or an ape perched in a palanquin,
Look on in silence. Quickly pass by.
Quickly.

Lenrie Peters

Born at Bathurst, Gambia, in 1932. He was educated at Bathurst,
Freetown and Cambridge, where he took a medical degree in
1959. He is now studying surgery in England.

Parachute

Parachute men say
The first jump
Takes the breath away
Feet in the air disturbs
Till you get used to it

Solid ground
Is now where you left it
As you plunge down
Perhaps head first
As you listen to
Your arteries talking
You learn to sustain hope

Suddenly you are only
Holding an open umbrella
In a windy place
As the warm earth
Reaches out to you
Reassures you
The vibrating interim is over

You try to land
Where green grass yields
And carry your pack
Across the fields

The violent arrival
Puts out the joint
Earth has nowhere to go
You are at the starting point

Jumping across worlds
In condensed time
After the awkward fall
We are always at the starting point.

Jean-Joseph Rabearivelo

Born at Antananarivo, Madagascar, in 1901, of poor parents.
With very little formal schooling he taught himself French and
Spanish and he wrote poetry in both these languages as well as
in his native Malagasy. He worked as a publisher's clerk and
published several volumes of poetry of which *Presque Songes* and
Traduit de la Nuit are the most important. In spite of his devotion
to French culture he was never able to visit France. He com-
mitted suicide in 1937. His *Vieilles Chansons du Pays d'Imerina*
was published after his death. These are prose poems in French
adapted from traditional Malagasy *hain-teny* (see Flavien Ranaivo).
He was co-editor of an interesting but short-lived literary review,
Capricorne (1930–31).

What you have done

'What have you done but listen to songs?
   What have you done yourself but sing?
   You have not listened to what men had to say,
   You have not spoken yourself.

'What books have you read,
   Except books that preserve the voices of women
   And unreal things?

'You have sung but you have not spoken
   You have not questioned the heart of things
   And you are unable to know them.'
Say the speakers and the scribes
Who laugh to see you magnify
The daily miracle of sea and sky.

But still you sing
   Wondering at the stem

That seeks an uncharted way
Over the slack sea
Making for unknown gulfs.
Wondering to follow with your eyes that bird
Sure of its way across the deserts of the sky
Finding again in the wind
The paths that lead back to its native wood.

And the books you write
Rustle with unreal things—
Unreal because too real
Like dreams.

Translated from the French

Flute-players

Your flute,
Cut from the thighbone of a mighty bull,
Polished on the bleak hillsides
Scourged by the sun.
Her flute,
Cut from the reed that quivers in the wind
Pierced on the banks of running water
Drunken with moonlight dreams.

In the deeps of evening, play them together
As if to right the sphered canoe
Capsizing by the shores of sky
And keep it
From its doom.
But your plaintive incantations
Do they reach the wind-gods

And the earth-gods and the wood-gods
And the gods of sand?

Your flute
Draws out a note where the ear can catch the tread of a
    maddened bull
Pounding toward the desert
And pounding back
Burnt by thirst and hunger
Felled by fatigue
At the foot of the tree without shadow
Without fruit, without leaves.

Her flute
Is like a reed that bends beneath the weight of a passing
    bird—
Not a bird trapped by a child
Ruffling its feathers
But a bird lost from the flock
Looking at his reflection in running water
For comfort.

Your flute
And hers—
Longing for their past
In the songs of your grief.

Translated from the French

Cactus

That multitude of fused hands
Still offering flowers to the sky,

Multitude of fingerless hands
That the wind is never enough to sway,
They say a hidden spring
Wells in their unbroken palms;
They say that inner spring
Waters many thousands of cattle
And many wandering tribes
In the borders of the South.   10

Fingerless hands spurt from a spring,
Fused hands wreathe the sky.

Here,
When they still made the slopes of the city as green
As glimpses of moonlight dancing in the forests,
When they still cooled with their breezes the hillsides of
    Iarivo
Crouched like bulls after food,
Away to sheer rocks where even the goats cannot go
Lepers in finery of flowers
They drew apart to guard their springs.   20

Fathom the cave from which they have come
To find the source of the sickness that thins them
—Source cloudier than evening
And more distant than the dawn—
But you will know no more than I.
Blood of the earth, sweat of the stone
Seed of the wind
Flowing together in these palms
Have dissolved the fingers,
In their place put golden flowers.   30

I know a child,
Still a prince in the kingdom of God
Who would go on:
'And Fate took pity on the lepers,
And told them to plant their flowers
And to guard their springs
Far from cruel men.'

Translated from the French

Three Daybreaks

I

Have you seen the dawn go poaching
In night's orchard?
See she comes
Down eastern pathways
Overgrown with lilyblooms.
From head to foot she is splashed with milk
Like those children long ago suckled by heifers.
Her hands that carry a torch
Are blue and black like the lips of a girl
Eating mulberries.   10

Escaping one by one there fly before her
The birds she has taken in her traps.

II

Is it from the east or from the west
The first call comes? We do not know.
But now

In their huts transfixed by stars
And other assegais of the dark,
The cocks enumerate themselves,
Blowing into seashells
Answering on every side   20
Until the sleeper in the ocean comes again
Until the ascension of the lark
Who goes to meet him and the songs she carries
Are drenched in dew.

III

All the stars melt together
In the crucible of time,
Cooled in the sea
To a many-faced stone-block.
A dying lapidist, the Night,
Sets to work with all his heart   30
And all his grief to see his mills
Crumbling, crumbling,
Like ashes in the wind,
And with what loving care, he cuts the prism.

The craftsman on his own unnoticed grave
Sets up this monument of light.

Translated from the French

What invisible rat

What invisible rat,
Come out of the walls of the night

Gnaws the milk-cake of the moon?
In the morning
He will be gone
Leaving bloodstained marks of teeth.

In the morning,
Those who have been drunk all night
And those who have just left the gaming tables
Seeing the moon
Will mutter
'Whose is that sixpence
Rolling on the green table?'
'Ah!' will say one
'He had lost everything
So he killed himself!'

And they all will snigger
And stagger and fall.
The moon will be gone.
The rat will have dragged it into his hole.

Translated from the French

Spider

Slow
As a limping cow
Or a mighty bull
Four times houghed,
A great black spider comes out of the earth
And climbs up the wall
Then painfully sets his back against the trees,

Throws out his threads for the wind to carry
Weaves a web that reaches the sky
And spreads his nets across the blue.   10

Where are the many-coloured birds?
Where are the precentors of the sun?
—Lights burst from their sleep-deadened eyes
Among their liana-swings
Reviving their dreams and their reverberations
In that shimmering of glow-worms
That becomes a cohort of stars,
And turns the spider's ambush
Which the horns of a bounding calf will tear.

Translated from the French

Two Old Merina songs

I

There in the north there stand two stones and they are
somewhat alike. One is black and the other is white. If I
take the white one, I am ashamed of the black. If I take the
black one, I am ashamed of the white. If I take them both,
one is love, the other consolation.

II

A wife is like a blade of grass. She stands upright but
easily withers.

A husband is like a tuft of seaweed growing confined
beneath the water and easily broken.

... Young man, how many lovers have you.

... My cousin, I have scarcely any lovers for my lovers are no more than seven; the first is the lover that cuts my nails; the second is the lover who takes the place of the one with us in the house, when I am away from home; the third takes her place in an emergency; the fourth is the lover who follows me with her eyes when I go away; the fifth is the lover who comes to meet me when I return; the sixth is the lover who sustains my life like rice; the seventh is the lover who does not mix with the crowd and even when she happens to be amongst them always knows how to make herself distinguished.

Translated from the French

Jacques Rabémananjara

Born in 1913 in Antananarivo, Madagascar. He was condemned to death for his alleged part in the 1947 uprising, later reprieved and exiled to France. He returned to Madagascar in 1960 as Minister of Economic Affairs. He is the author of several plays and volumes of poetry, most of which glorify the Malagasy past and its culture. *L'éventail du rêve; Aux confins de la Nuit; Sur les Marches du Soir* (1942); *Les Dieux Malgaches* (1947); *Antsa* (1956); *Rites millénaires* (1956); *Lamba* (1956); *Les Boutriers de l'Aurore* (1957); *Antidote* (1961); *Agapes des Dieux* (1962).

Blue, blue, the eye of heaven

Blue, blue, the eye of heaven
  Beyond the window!
Life in blossom between my lashes
Unbroken sky between my lids.

61

Blue, blue, the eye of heaven
   Beyond the window!

Bleak, bleak, these four walls.
Death impregnates earth and stone
With a cold otherworldly sweat.
Fresh, fresh, the children's shouts
   In the courtyard.

But who will hear, bright Innocence
   A song so pure
   A voice so soft
In the uproar of the night?

Blind force of the abyss
   Draws from this whip
The sour sound of pain.
Suffering's tender skin
Bleeds at the hard kiss of the cord.

Stars die unsighingly.
At the horizon what raised hand
Will lift to the hero's lips
The red offering of Dawn?

Blood I have not shed.
Death I have not sown.
My fingers are clean as springtime.
My heart new as a host.

But who will hear, chaste warrior,
   A voice so pure,
   A song so soft
In the cawing of the dark?

Blue, blue, the eye of heaven
  Behind the bars.
Fresh, fresh, the children's cries
  On the lawn.
Life in blossom between my lashes.
Unbroken sky between my lids.
Innocence between the folds of my heart . . .

               Translated from the French

Flavien Ranaivo

Born in 1914 at Arivonimamo, Madagascar. His poetry is
deeply influenced by the *hain-teny*—a traditional Malagasy poetic
dialogue, generally on a love-theme. Since the creation of the
Malagasy Republic in 1960 he has been the Director of Information. He has published three volumes of poetry: *L'Ombre et le
Vent* (1947); *Mes Chansons de toujours* (1955) and *Le Retour au
bercail* (1962).

Popular Love-Song

Do not love me, my cousin
Like your shadow
For at nightfall shadows vanish
And I must keep watch for you
Until the cocks crow;
Nor like pepper
That warms the belly
For what should I use
To take off hunger?
Nor like your pillow   10

63

Together through the hours of sleep
In the daytime hardly meeting;
Nor like rice
No sooner eaten than forgotten;
Nor like sweet words
That vanish into air;
Nor like honey
Sweet but commonplace.
Love me like a good dream,
Your life at night-time 20
My hope in daytime;
Like a piece of silver,
On land not to be parted from
And on a long voyage
A faithful companion;
Or like the gourd,
Whole, it fetches water,
Broken, the pieces make bridges for valihas.

Translated from the French

Carry Me

Carry me
Carry me, O feet of mine
To join the road
The road that runs there under cover
Of the thick and flickering leaves.
It is a great while since I saw
My father and my mother.

Translated from the French

Choice

Who is that making her steps clatter on the firm earth?
—She is the daughter of the new chief-over-a-thousand
—If she is the daughter of the chief-over-a-thousand,
Tell her night will soon be falling
And I would trade all the coral-red loves
For a hint of her friendship.

—Who is she coming from the north?
—It is the sister of the widow scented with rose-apples.
—Tell her to come inside at once,
I will make her a fine dinner.
—She will not touch it I know:
She will take a little rice-water
Not because she is thirsty
But because it is her whim to please you.

Translated from the French

Zebu

His lips move unceasingly
But they are not swollen or worn;
His teeth are two fine rows of coral;
His horns form a circle
Which is never closed.
His eyes: two immense pearls shining in the night;
His hump is Mount-Abundance
His tail lashes the air
But is not more than half a fly-switch;
His body is a well-filled coffer
On four dry sticks.

Translated from the French

Traditional Theme from Merina

The plants grow
Driven by their roots
And driven by my love I come to you.

At the top of the tall trees, my dear
The bird ends his flight:
My ways find ending only when I am close to you.

The waters of Farahantsana, my dear, tumble, tumble
They fall, they fall but are not broken.

My love for you my dear
Is like the water by the bank: 10
When I expect it to dry up, it grows deeper.

Two loves have grown up together
Like two twin loves.
Grief come to the first who is untrue.

Goodbye, my dear, goodbye.
Foolish love deceives the eye,
Unsettled love drives to madness.

For foolish love
Is like mist on a pool
So much but nothing your hand can grasp.   20
For mist on the pool my dear
Touches you and is gone.
Avoko stands rooted on the borders of the fields.

The chicken seized by the papango, my dear
See, carried so high it grows lonely
See, up in the sky it is far from its love.

Morning nostalgia dulls the mind;
Nostalgia in daytime is tiring;
Evening nostalgia is sweetest—my dear, which nostalgia is
   yours?

Our relationship, my dear,   30
A grain of sand in the eye;
Small but it dazes your sight.

Our relationship, my dear,
Silt slowly gathering
That becomes a house of bricks.

Hurry then hurry
Hurry my dear
In case night overtakes you.

My legs are broken
My eyes see dimly   40
My dear, tell them down there that I can do no more.

What if the twilight covers the earth,
My heart is beneath an eternal moonlight:
So come to my side.

I shall be grumbled at home.
My elder sister does not want me to go with you,
But what do I care about that.

I would like to, but I cannot
I am in love, but I am afraid . . .
I will come, but come with me my dear.   50

The door is shut, my dear,
You have come too late, my love,
I shall be grumbled at home.

Open the door, I will tell you secrets
Open the door, and let us talk.
Open the door. I love you.

The door is shut, my dear,
But my heart is open.
Come in my cousin. I love you.

Your door—is it not made of zozoro reeds?   60
Why then should you lock it?
Open the door, for I am tired of waiting.

Translated from the French

David Rubadiri

Born in 1930, in Malawi (Nyasaland). Studied English at
Makerere College, Kampala, Uganda. He was arrested and de-
tained by the government when a state of emergency was declared
in Nyasaland in 1959. After his release he went to England and
studied English at Cambridge University. Since his return he
has worked in the Ministry of Education and is now teaching.

Stanley meets Mutesa

Such a time of it they had;
The heat of the day
The chill of the night
And the mosquitoes that followed.
Such was the time and
They bound for a kingdom.

The thin weary line of carriers
With tattered dirty rags to cover their backs;

The battered bulky chests
That kept on falling off their shaven heads.   10
Their tempers high and hot
The sun fierce and scorching
With it rose their spirits
With its fall their hopes
As each day sweated their bodies dry and
Flies clung in clumps on their sweat-scented backs.
Such was the march
And the hot season just breaking.

Each day a weary pony dropped,
Left for the vultures on the plains;   20
Each afternoon a human skeleton collapsed,
Left for the Masai on the plains;
But the march trudged on
Its Khaki leader in front
He the spirit that inspired.
He the light of hope.

Then came the afternoon of a hungry march,
A hot and hungry march it was;
The Nile and the Nyanza
Lay like two twins   30
Azure across the green countryside.
The march leapt on chaunting
Like young gazelles to a water hole.
Hearts beat faster
Loads felt lighter
As the cool water lapt their sore soft feet.
No more the dread of hungry hyenas
But only tales of valour when
At Mutesa's court fires are lit.

No more the burning heat of the day 40
But song, laughter and dance.

The village looks on behind banana groves,
Children peer behind reed fences.
Such was the welcome
No singing women to chaunt a welcome
Or drums to greet the white ambassador;
Only a few silent nods from aged faces
And one rumbling drum roll
To summon Mutesa's court to parley
For the country was not sure. 50

The gate of reeds is flung open,
There is silence
But only a moment's silence—
A silence of assessment.
The tall black king steps forward,
He towers over the thin bearded white man
Then grabbing his lean white hand
Manages to whisper
'Mtu Mweupe karibu'
White man you are welcome. 60
The gate of polished reed closes behind them
And the west is let in.

A Negro Labourer in Liverpool

I have passed him
Slouching on dark backstreet pavements
Head bowed—

Taut, haggard and worn.
A dark shadow amidst dark shadows.

I have lifted my face to his,
Our eyes met
But on his dark negro face
No sunny smile,
No hope or longing for a hope promised;
Only the quick cowed dart of eyes
Piercing through impassive crowds
Searching longingly for a face
Feeling painfully for a heart
That might flicker understanding.

This is him—
The negro labourer in Liverpool
That from his motherland,
A heart heavy
With the load of a century's oppression,
Gloriously sought for an identity
Grappled to clutch the fire of manhood
In the land of the free.
But here are only the free dead—
For they too are groping for a light.

Will that sun
That greeted him from his mother's womb
Ever shine again?
Not here—
Here his hope is the shovel,
And his fulfilment resignation.

Léopold Sédar Senghor

Born in 1906 at Joal, Senegal. He is a Serer. He was educated at Dakar and then in Paris at the Lycée Louis-le-Grand and the Sorbonne. He taught French in high schools in France before the war. At the outbreak of war he enlisted and was for some time a prisoner-of-war in Germany. Many of his early poems were inspired by this experience. After the war he taught in the *École Nationale de la France d'outre-mer*, where his subject was African languages. He entered politics and as a Deputy in the French Parliament and leader of an important group of African politicians in West Africa, he played a leading part in obtaining independence for the French African colonies. Since 1960 he has been the President of the Senegalese Republic. He has written on political topics, on the concept of *négritude*, and compiled an important anthology of French poetry by Africans and men of African descent, the *Anthologie de la nouvelle poésie nègre et malgache* (1948). His volumes of poetry are *Chants d'ombre* (1945); *Hosties Noires* (1948); *Chants pour Naëtt* (1949); *Éthiopiques* (1956) and *Nocturnes* (1961).

All day long

All day long along the long straight rails
(Unbending will on the listless sands)
Across the dryness of Cayor and Baol where the arms of
    the baobabs twist in anguish
All day long, all along the line
Through tiny stations, each exactly like the last, chattering
    little black girls uncaged from school
All day long, roughly shaken on the benches of the clanking,
    dust-covered wheezing, antique train
I come seeking to forget about Europe in the pastoral heart
    of Sine.

Translated from the French

Mother, they have written you are turning white, as the bush turns white at the end of the rains

When I should be your festival, gymnic feast for your harvests

Your fair season, with the unclouded seven times nine years, and the barns full to bursting with fine millet

Your champion *Kor-Sanou*! Like the palmtree of Katamague

Head and swaying silver plume above all his rivals

And the woman's hair fluttering at their shoulders and the hearts of the maidens in the tumult of their breasts.

I am here, Mother before you, a soldier in shirt sleeves,

Dressed up in foreign words, where your eyes see only a set of sticks and tatters

If I could tell you, Mother! But you would hear an affected prattle, you would not understand

As when good Serer women make mock of the god, herdsmen of clouds   10

With a rattle of rifle shots over the jingle of *paragnessé* words.

Speak to me Mother. My tongue slips on our sonorous hard words.

You can make them gentle and soft, as you made them once for the son you loved.

The pious burden of my lie is heavy upon me

I am no longer an official with authority, a marabout with delighted disciples,

Europe has broken me like a wretched soldier under the pachydermatous paws of tanks

My heart is more bruised than my body was once, home from adventures far off on the magical shores of the Spirits.

I should have been, Mother, the flourishing palm tree of your age, I would give you back the ecstasy of your young years.

Now I am only your little boy in pain, tossing and turning on his aching sides.   20

Now, I am only a little boy who remembers his mother's breast and cries.

Take me into the night that is lit by the confidence you are close

Tell me over again the old stories of black evenings so that I lose myself down roads without memory

Mother, I am a humbled soldier, fed with coarse millet.

Tell me the pride of my fathers.

Translated from the French

Taga for Mbaye Dyob

(*for a tama*)

Mbaye Dyob! I will speak your name and your honour.

Dyob! I will hoist your name to the. high mast of the ship returning, ring your name like the bell that sounds victory,

I will sing your name Dyobene! you who called me master and

Warmed me with your fervour in the winter evenings around the red stove that made us cold.

Dyob! You cannot trace back your ancestry and bring order into black history, your forefathers are not sung by the voice of the tama.

You who have never killed a rabbit, who went to ground
under the bombs of the great vultures
Dyob! you who are not captain or airman or trooper, not
even in the baggage train,
But a second-class private in the Fourth Regiment of the
Senegal Rifles
Dyob, I will celebrate your white honour.

The girls of Gandyol will make you a triumphal arch with
their curved arms, arms of silver and of red gold   10
Make you a path of glory with their precious cloths from
the rivers of the South.
Then they will make you with their mouths a necklace of
ivory, better to wear than a royal garment
Then they will cradle your steps, their voices will mingle
with the waves of the sea
Then they will sing 'You have faced more than death, more
than the tanks and the planes that defy all magic
'You have faced hunger, you have faced cold, and the
humiliation of captivity.
'O bravely, you have been the footstool of griots and clowns
'You have put new nails in your cross so as not to desert
your companions
'Not to break the unspoken pact
'Not to leave your load to your comrades, whose backs bend
at each new start
'Whose arms grow weak each evening when there is one
less hand to shake   20
'And the face grows darker lit by one less look, the eyes
sunken, reflecting one less smile.'
Dyob! from Ngabu to the Walo, from Ngalam to the sea
will rise the songs of the amber virgins

75

Let them be accompanied by strings of the kora, let them be accompanied by the waves and the winds
Dyob! I speak your name and your honour.

Translated from the French

To the American Negro Soldiers

I did not recognise you in your prison of sad-coloured uniforms
I did not recognise you under that calabash helmet with no plume
I did not recognise the quavering whinny of your iron horses that drink but do not eat.
No longer the nobility of elephants but the barbaric clumsiness of monsters from the foretime of the world.
Under your closed faces I did not recognise you.
I only touched the warmth of your brown hand. I said my name, 'Afrika!'
And found again lost laughter, I greeted the ancient voice and the roar of the cascades of the Congo.
Brothers, I do not know if it was you who bombed the cathedrals, the pride of Europe
If you are the lightning that in God's hand burnt Sodom and Gomorrah.
No, you are the messengers of his mercy, breath of Spring after Winter.
For those who had forgotten laughter (using only an oblique smile)
Who had forgotten the salt taste of tears and the irritant smell of blood
You bring the springtime of Peace, hope at the end of waiting

And their night fills with a sweetness of milk, the blue fields
of the sky covered with flowers, softly the silence sings.
You bring the sun. The air throbs with liquid murmurs and
crystalline whistling and the silky beat of wings
Aerial cities are warm with nests.
Down streets running with joy, boys play with their dreams
Men dance before their machines, and catch themselves
singing.
The eyelids of schoolgirls are rose petals, fruits ripen at the
breasts of virgins
The hips of the women . . . o sweetness . . . grow full and
heavy.
Black brothers, warriors whose mouths are singing flowers
. . . O delight to live after Winter . . . I greet you as the
messengers of peace.

Translated from the French

Message

They sent me a swift courier
He crossed the violence of rivers, in the low rice-fields he
waded up to the navel.
It meant that their message was urgent.
I left my meal still steaming and my attention to many law-
suits.
Just a cloth. I took nothing against the dewy mornings.
Provisions for the journey, white words of peace to open
the way for me everywhere.
I too crossed the rivers, and the virgin ambushes of the
forests,

Where lianas hung down, more treacherous than serpents.
I passed through the tribes that let fly a poisonous greeting.
But I did not lose the sign of my recognition   10
And the spirits watched over the breath of my nostrils.
I recognised the ashes of former camps, I recognised the
    hereditary hosts.
We exchanged long speeches under the kailcedrats
We exchanged the ritual gifts.
And I came to Elissa, nest of falcons defying the Invader's
    pride.
I saw once more the ancient dwelling on the hillside, a
    village with its long lowered eyelashes
To the Guardians of the Blood I recited the long message.
Murrain. Ruin of trade. Game laws. Middle-class respect-
    ability
The dry contempt that swells the bellies of captives.   [20
The Prince answered. This is the exact imprint of his words
'Children how short your memories are. What did the koras
    sing to you?
'You decline the rose, I hear, and your ancestors are the
    Gauls.
'You are doctors of the Sorbonne, pot-bellied with degrees
'You amass scraps of paper—not even golden louis to count
    under the lamp like your father with his griping fingers
'Your daughters I hear paint their faces like prostitutes
'Through their promiscuous loves, our race grows paler.
'Are you any happier? Some trumpet goes wa wa wa
'And down there in the evenings you weep great fires and
    blood.
'Must the ancient drama, the epic be unfolded to you,
'Go to M'Bissel to Fa'oy. Recite the rosary of the sanctuaries
    which mark out the Great Way   30

'Take again the Royal Route. Meditate this Way of the Cross
  and of Glory.
'Your high priests will answer you. Voice of Blood.
'More lovely than the palm trees are the Dead of Elissa,
  few were the wants of their bellies
'Their shield of honour never left them nor their loyal lance.
'They did not hoard up rags, or even guineas to adorn their
  dolls.
'Their flocks covered and hid their lands, such were their
  dwellings in the divine shadow of the fig-trees.
'And their barns were packed to bursting with the harvest
  of children.
'Voice of Blood! Things to be thought on!
'The conquerors will greet your step. Your children will be
  the white cross of your head.'
I heard the words of the Prince.   40
Herald of the Good News, such was his ivory message.

Translated from the French

Martial Sinda

Born near Brazzaville, Congo Republic. He studied in Brazzaville
and Paris and he has published one volume of verse: *Premier
Chant du Départ* (1956).

You will walk in peace

You will walk in peace
    Through the night,
    When you go,

79

N'dila ho, do not listen
To the voices of the owls
Because
They tell of death.

You will walk in peace.
Through the night
On your way, N'dila ho
If you meet a mole
If you smell a certain root
Used when bodies are embalmed
What they foretell is death.

You will sleep in peace
Through the night.
If you hear your name
If you hear a low knock on your door
Never never never answer
For
Death is watching you.

You will always be in peace,
O N'dila ho, if you sneeze
During the day;
At night,
Sneezing is an evil sign.

Translated from the French

Wole Soyinka

Nigerian poet and playwright, born at Abeokuta, Nigeria, in 1935. Studied at University College, Ibadan, and read for an English Honours degree at Leeds University. He returned to Nigeria in 1960, and is now on the staff of the University of Ife. His plays have been produced by the Masks Dramatic Group in Ibadan, and two of them, *A Dance of the Forests* and *The Lion and the Jewel*, have been published by the Oxford University Press (1963).

Telephone Conversation

The price seemed reasonable, location
Indifferent. The landlady swore she lived
Off premises. Nothing remained
But self-confession. 'Madam,' I warned,
'I hate a wasted journey—I am—African.'
Silence. Silenced transmission of
Pressurised good-breeding. Voice, when it came,
Lip-stick coated, long gold-rolled
Cigarette-holder pipped. Caught I was, foully.
'HOW DARK?' . . . I had not misheard . . . 'ARE YOU
    LIGHT   10
OR VERY DARK?' Button B. Button A. Stench
Of rancid breath of public-hide-and-speak.
Red booth. Red pillar-box. Red double-tiered
Omnibus squelching tar. It *was* real! Shamed
By ill-mannered silence, surrender
Pushed dumbfoundment to beg simplification.
Considerate she was, varying the emphasis—
'ARE YOU DARK? OR VERY LIGHT?' Revelation came.
'You mean—like plain or milk chocolate?'
Her assent was clinical, crushing in its light   20

Impersonality. Rapidly, wave-length adjusted,
I chose, 'West African sepia'—and as an afterthought,
'Down in my passport.' Silence for spectroscopic
Flight of fancy, till truthfulness clanged her accent
Hard on the mouthpiece. 'WHAT'S THAT?' conceding
'DON'T KNOW WHAT THAT IS.' 'Like brunette.'
'THAT'S DARK, ISN'T IT?' 'Not altogether.
'Facially, I am brunette, but madam, you should see
The rest of me. Palm of my hand, soles of my feet
Are a peroxide blond. Friction, caused—   30
Foolishly madam—by sitting down, has turned
My bottom raven black—One moment madam!'—sensing
Her receiver rearing on the thunder clap
About my ears—'Madam,' I pleaded, 'Wouldn't you rather
See for yourself?'

U. I. Ukwu

Nigerian. Studied at University College (now the University of
Ibadan) and Caius College, Cambridge.

A Bus Ride

Two ample women, somewhat past their primes
(the man between lost in his *Daily Times*)
discuss their friends for all the world to hear.
Some seats away a gallant says, 'My dear'
to a strange girl, who glares at him. Uncowed
he prattles on, oblivious of the crowd.
On every side there's animated talk
on the state, on love—down to the price of pork.

Some stare through windows, hating all the noise,
Stern-faced, like masters angry with their boys.
The fop uneasy with the tramp beside
fidgets and sighs and shifts from side to side.

A bus stop now.
Sighs and farewells, legs and baskets,
jostle in greatest confusion.
The queue without stampedes and rushes
t'increase the babel within.
'Way please!' 'Get in!' 'Abi na wetin!'
'Ouch, you've hurt my toe!'

Time up! The bus conductor presses 'Go'.
The hubbub continues. What does he care?
The more the noisier, but the richer the fare!

James J. R. Jolobe

Born at Lovedale in the Cape Province of South Africa, by tribe
a Xhosa. He studied at Fort Hare University and became a
minister of the Presbyterian Church. He is well known as a poet
in his own language and has published a volume of translations
into English of his own Xhosa poems. (*Poems of an African*
(1946).) The English version of *Thuthula* from this volume is
here given in a slightly shortened form.

Thuthula

This song of mine at far Xhukwane starts,
Around the district of the Xesi stream,
Nor far from the Mathole mountain slopes.

Here dwelt the offspring of Chief Phalo great,
In house polygamous the right-hand sons
Illustrious chief Rarabe and his tribe.

Those days the custom of the tribe did rule.
Large herds of cattle were the goal supreme,
The cows did yield of milk, the gourds were filled,
Men bred the racing oxen for their sport;
They wedded wives, and there were nuptial feasts.
Of daughters, too, the mothers were most proud,
And so of youth the thoughtful aged men.

There lived in that far place a certain man,
A tribesman true he was at Gaxa's home.
This man a daughter beautiful he had
Who was as sweet in spirit as in mind.
She was sixteen when we begin this tale,
Just like a bud beginning to unfold.
In household craft she had been tutored well,   20
Like all the growing maids among the tribe,
To plaster dwelling walls, to hoe the lands.
They were acquainted with the distant woods,
Although they were never at home in these,
For all believed, the aged and the young,
That here there lived some creatures passing strange,
With maiden faces beautiful to view.
Whoever saw them had to pay by death.
The shades of the departed in the tribe,
The legend said they could be seen at times.
As sole protection from these dangers quaint
Was trust and hope and faith unwavering
In that great power invisible to eye,

Belief passed down from father to the son
That spirits of their ancestors had guard
O'er those who kept the custom of the tribe;
For verily in this their darkness deep
Of mind and soul, in which they lived and died,
A ray of hope there was—Qamata great,
The first among all things—creator too,   40
And hence they skyward pointed with closed hand.

One day—and woe the day—this maiden sweet,
In company with other damsels young,
Was in these forests fuel to collect.
The summer sun shone clear, and great the heat,
And, when her bundle of the wood had tied,
To quench her thirst a cooling spring she sought.
So first some blades of grass into the spring
She cast as charm, and then knelt down to drink.
On rising up, she saw a greyhound cross
The streamlet from the spring. A hunter young
Behind the dog was following. He was
A youth in stature tall, and straight of limb,
With noble face and handsome to behold.

The maiden's heart did beat and leap and ache,
And fittingly it did, for she had seen
The lion's cub—Chief Mlawu's son the prince,
A hunter even in those early days
At his paternal uncle's home and realm.
When he espied this maiden beautiful,   60
Mthunzana's daughter, Thuthula by name,
Exclaiming joyfully he said, 'My heart!
O! little dusky maid, of thirst I die.

How is the water, O my mother's child?'
Then answered she and said 'Cool is the spring.'
At once she called to other maids to come
In sport to make him choose his favourite
Among them, but he felt confused, poor boy!
Surrounded by these beauties of the race.
At last with diffidence he made his choice.
On beautiful Thuthula fell the lot.
With one accord all said it could not well
Be otherwise, and all in jest it was.
The youth in earnest now asked for her name;
When told, the prince did briefly give her thanks.
His heart was warmed, he kept the name in mind.
Their tender souls had shaken hands that hour,
For love is old as this gaunt world of ours.
Our souls were made in twos like unto twins.
In life there is a search, a quest, a hunt—   80
One twin goes out to seek for its twin mate,
For long ago it was proclaimed and said,
'It is not good that man should be alone.
Now let us make a helping mate for him.'
The twin mate, we believe, was meant by this.
The day the power of love assails a man
That day he's tracked his soul twin and the mate.
This thing called love is sacred, holy, pure.
It is the better self—man's complement.
It is a thing of worth, a royal gift,
More precious than all else we greatly prize.
No bar nor gulf should ever rise between
Two hearts, two souls, two twins that yearn in love
For one another's company on earth.
As so it was with this young man this day.

And when the maids wished then his name to know,
With royal mien he answered in this wise:
His name was Ngqika, Mlawu's son, a prince
Born of Rarabe, son in right-hand house
Of Phalo's—king of the MaXhosa tribe.   100
And, having spoken, thence he moved away
With whistle sharp that pierced the drowsy noon,
His prowling greyhound calling back to him.
He never turned to cast a backward glance,
And yet we know he was no longer whole.
His heart was stolen by Thuthula's charm.
He felt within the depths of his young heart
Some thoughts and longings like a painful joy.

And from that day Thuthula too was changed;
She felt a different maid in mind and heart,
She longed and yearned for something undefined.
The picture of this noble Xhosa prince
Kept flitting through the mind of this young maid;
His voice was ever sounding in her ears,
And beckoning, inviting her to joy.
But days and months and years rolled by without
These two again finding a chance to meet.
The flame however, kindled at that spring
In neither of them was allowed to die.

II

But note, the times are not in human hands.   120
Each one is born a task to do on earth
Which only he must do, nobody else,
To further and advance God's plan on earth.

With some the day is full of heat and toil,
A stormy day with others on the road;
For others still the giddy heights to climb,
But when the finger points and bids us go
We must obey and face the task with joy,
For cowardice it is to turn our backs.
That finger stern directed Mlawu's son
Prince Ngqika to assume the royal staff.
The councillors did urge him to this claim.
He rode astride upon this wave; and like
A riding ox, it carried him apace
To worlds for which the hearts of men do yearn,
Supremacy and power and honour sweet,
And Yese's party backed this royal claim,
Recalling well the day Chief Khawuta came,
And placed around his neck the royal beads,
Henceforth all things in order seemed to be.   140
The lion's cub soon went into his rights
As king. All said, 'Lwaganda, hail to thee.'

    'The Tshulubembe great,
      Who laughs until the last.
      The wooden pole for gate
      At Phalo's cattle fold.
The ring-tailed monkey of the Nkwebus.
      The black serpent,
      Which crosses pools.
The vulture with the dark brown wings.'

It was not long when muffled cries were raised:
Amaphakathi said chief Ndlambe proud,
The regent chief, was rivalling the king.
No harmony nor peace can ever dwell

Where there is found two bulls in single fold.
Then Regent Ndlambe crossed the Nxuba flood
At Alexandria to make a home,
In regions round the Sundays River belt
Just where it winds its way into the sea;
And in those jungles wild they made a home   160
And dwelt with game, with beast and elephant.
Among the tribe of this the regent chief
Was old Mthunzana with his family,
Thuthula too, their daughter, was with them.

Those days the chief vocation of the maids
It was to marry, find a lord and home.
Lobola cows were paid for virgin maids.
To gain this end the mothers too did strive
To guard and foster innocence of maids.
Alas! again because of this same end
Their happiness was often sacrificed
To loveless marriages without a choice.
One day out there at this Mthunzana's kraal
A spear, betrothal's sign, was left in court.
Report was made it came from royal kraal.
The chief, the regent Ndlambe at this time,
Had wives who did not number less than ten;
A wife for his old age now wanted he;
He saw this little dove, this charming maid;
He fell in love, and never stopped to ask   180
Where lay her heart, nor tried to win her love.
The master of the ceremonies too
As middle man between the parties worked.
A royal *khazi* in a day was paid.
Thuthula felt that loneliness which comes

To one who knows a secret known to none,
Which none can understand if told perchance,
And in the depths of her young heart there was
A wail which issued from a saddened soul,
And seemed in groping yearning words to say,

'By night on my bed
I sought him whom my soul loveth.
I sought him but I found him not.
I will arise now,
And go about the city in the streets
And in the broad way.
I will seek him whom my soul loveth.
I sought him and found him not.'

Then married they in ancient style approved.
There were *mphothulo* and *inqhakhwe* cows,   200
And also famous *ubulunga* beast.
And the *ingqongqo* drum was sounded loud
By women of the race, the Xhosa dames.
Hence row did follow row of men abreast,
With a staff in hand *umdudo* has begun,
Anon the active *ngqaqhu* step succeeds
A line of leaping, dancing younger men.
The last step, *umtyhulubo*, now does sound,
Men quiver here like reeds on river bank.
All this was done this day to place a seal
And witness to the wedding of these two.
Such was the marriage of Thuthula sweet.
She thus became the wife of Ndlambe bold.
With life around she seemed to be in death;
To her life seemed an empty honeycomb,
Because of her soul-twin, the man she loved.

III

Our life is full of change, new things occur;
Although some say there's nothing new on earth,
What may to us seem old elsewhere is new.
A beast itself that roams the pastures wild   220
Is shy confronted with an object strange;
It sniffs and rears and sniffs again, with aim
To know and classify experience new,
And so is man in face of things unknown.

A certain man, Ntsikana, Gaba's son,
At break of day he saw a vision bright;
The sun that morn on his Hulushe struck
An ox which was a favourite to him.
The Sun of Righteousness on him perhaps
While yet a boy in bygone days had struck,
When Van der Kemp the messenger made known
The Tidings of the Lord—Evangel true.

And from this day Ntsikana, Gaba's son,
In heart, in mind, in soul no peace found he.
The Hound of Heaven, like *inqhina* band,
Was tracking down his soul, as hounds the game.
He did attend a dance that day, we hear,
But in his blanket closely wrapped he sat
In meditation, none suspecting that
The mighty power of God had passed o'er him.   240
His mates did call, inviting him to come
And join them in the dancing step. They said:

> 'Here is pleasure, Nokhonongo.
> Here is pleasure, Nokhonongo,
>   O thou secret man.'

But he refused and still they called again.
At last he rose in readiness to dance.
The Grace of God, however, intervened,
As if an angel waved its wings with might,
A whirlwind strong did rush across the court
And down he sat. He had not raised a foot.
In course of time again he stood to dance:
The mighty wind once more did rush and blow.
Ntsikana grave responded to his call.
His goods he now collects and gives command
To his dear wives with him home to return.
Forthwith he cleansed himself of ochre red,
And uttered some strange things by word of mouth.
He said, 'This thing I hear says we must pray.'
He raised his voice, appealing to his tribe   260
To shun all evil and embrace the good.

When Ngqika heard a messenger he sent
Jothelo's son, named Soga—councillor—
And Jwara, when he came was wonderstruck
With what he saw and what he heard by ear.
Lwaganda called Ntsikana to his court.
To pitch his hut at Thwathwa gave him site.
From there he called the nation to his God;
But men of state the councillors did hate
To hear this wondrous message fresh from heaven
With no avail, for Ngqika the great king
Had caught a spark. His heart was quite aflame.
He said: 'I must be first to lead my tribe.'
At Ncera by the Tyume stream he had
A cattle post to which he went to nurse
The call from God, and the surrounding hills

Increased the flame in meditation lone,
When roaming among the solitary hills
Whose beauty brings warm rapture to the soul,
I-Ntab'eGqira and the Hogsback mount,   280
With rocky foreheads raised to view the plains
And forests like a man with bushy face,
Relieved by streamlets making tiny falls
Like milk for ever pouring from a gourd,
The sight of these child falls when seen afar.
Among these stately mountains he did roam
The chief Lwaganda at this time of change.
Amaphakathi staid were moved with fear
When they beheld the Gospel's power at work.
They were not ready yet for any change
In ancient order, custom, life and faith.
For counsel fresh in secret some did meet
To find a way to kill this strange new thing.
Alas! this Truth for ever dogged by hate
Though muffled it shall never be by man.
At Babylon was not a furnace made?
And yet amid its flames it stalked unharmed.
To kill it Herod, too, at Palestine
By Massacre of Innocents did try.
At Calvary did they not once exult   300
With hope of triumph over this same Truth?
And yet it rose victorious over death.

Among the Xhosas this same course they took.
One said the source was this Ntsikana wild,
And Ngqika too the chief had been enmeshed.
They must be cut; the message too should die.
When ways and means were asked from those who spoke,

They said: 'They must be punished, as is fit,
By one of blood, by Ndlambe regent chief.
The cause of war, his wife, the favourite—
The beautiful Thuthula—we must steal.
Be sure a war will break as ne'er was seen,
For by our custom this is evil base.'
They must have whispered into Ngqika's ear,
To gain the chief's connivance; said to him,
'The famous beauty, dame Thuthula sweet,
Is fit to be a spouse to thee, great chief.'
And thus did touch the king at his weak spot
As one who loved supremacy and power;
And thus again they did revive the fire   320
Of love, which was well-nigh extinguished then,
The forest spark enkindled long ago.
The chief therefore did lightly give consent,
Not realising that a trap was laid.

IV

And hence there left one day two messengers,
Two days they travelled on their journey long
And on the third day reached chief Ndlambe's realm.
They lodged and boarded with the tribesmen kind.
At dusk one day their secret task to do
Their steps they set towards the chief's great place.

And there the dog did bark and never ceased.
'And wherefore does this dog bark so tonight?'
Someone replies, to still the fears and doubts,
'This creature ever an alarmist was.'
But still another voice is heard to say,
'By yesternight for sure an owl did hoot

In this the royal kraal on top of hut.'
The dog still barking, then a certain boy
As he beyond the kraal by chance did walk,
He heard a whisper calling him. He looked   340
And there he saw the men behind a bush.
They asked him if he knew Thuthula sweet,
And then commanded him to summon her
To come, as there were men who wished to see
Her soon, but asked him no one else to tell.
In truth it was not long before she came;
Some distance off she stood and greeted them,
And they the greeting in low tone returned.
She asked about their health, and they in turn,
And whence they came. They said from Tyume far,
And then they asked if she were happy here.
She was a wedded wife, and was, she said,
Quite happy, but they said they here were sent.

Forthwith a fear did seize this woman poor,
At once she felt quite sure without a doubt
That some disaster strange would fall on her,
And yet she did not know what kind it was.
She asked the name of him who sent them there.
They said 'Lwaganda, Chief and Paramount,
To come and bring you to his kraal and realm,   360
For sad is he in heart because of thee.'
Then answered she and said, 'I cannot leave
This kraal, my home; I am a wedded wife.
I am Mthunzana's daughter, as you know,
And am a royal wife at Gaxa's home,
Will I desert this home? It cannot be!'
They said: 'Your chief, your king, your lord does call.

Yon Ndlambe's chief, the grandchild of the great
Rarabe. Yea, the lion's cub does call.'

A battle grim raged in the woman's heart.
This day, this night, her life entire was raised
From its deep grave where buried long it was.
The lover of her heart, her twin, her mate,
At last had come to claim her into life.
But woe is she! So tightly was she bound
In bonds of strength which were unbreakable.
She had to choose between this sacred vow
Of marriage called *umdudo*, and her love;
Between her pleasure and this holy thing.
Confused, disturbed, at last she only said,   380
'I cannot, sure, consider though I will.
If when the cock begins to crow tonight
I am not here with you, then know for sure
My choice is made, though bitter it may be.
Apologise, ask pardon from the chief,
And to his royal ear thus speak and say—
I am most thankful for this honour high
To stretch his hands and raise up from the dust
Even I, his servant maid, such as I am.
Moreover, this say you to him. The heart
Of his handmaiden here today is warm
Because of this the royal favour sweet.'
And then the beauty left the messengers.
She went not to the kraal but to a bush,
And sobbed with sorrow like a little child.
From there she sought her hut within the kraal
She laid herself to rest with beating heart,
Reviewing her past life in mind. At last

With sigh both deep and sad from troubled soul
She made her awful choice, and whispering said,   400
'I go. Beloved, here I come, I come.'
Then she disrobed herself of royal beads,
A loving gift from Ndlambe, regent chief.
She rolled them with the mat on which she lay,
And faced the darkness of that winter night.
And as she crossed the court of royal kraal
The cock did crow. A certain dog, mark you,
On haunches sat and faced the heavens dark,
And wailed a doleful howl as sad as death.
Thus went Thuthula, leaving Gaxa's home.

And so she went with these strange men from far.
Sweet liberty today she thought she had,
And yet in bondage stern in truth she was,
Her conscience now did wake, and troubled her.
The rustling of the grass as they did flee
Was like the steps of men pursuing her.
Her heart was terrified and beat apace.
Throughout that night a distance covered they;
At dawn they left the road and turned aside
To seek some roomy rocks to hide themselves,   420
For evil ever fears the light of day.
From hiding place they saw the morning sun
Rise up with shining rays of golden hue.
It kissed the distant hills until they smiled
Just like a babe caressed in mother's arms.
They saw it rise until noonday it was,
And all the while Thuthula soundly slept
And men by turns as sentinels kept watch.
At last it sank. Once more they took the road,

And on the second day of travel long,
This day they came to journey's end, they reached
The Tyume River famed for waters sweet.
They took Thuthula to old Ntlebi's kraal
And gave report to Chief Lwaganda grand.
His steed Ngqawane fast was brought with haste,
His heart and mind were set for Ntlebi's kraal,
And straight went he just where Thuthula was.
He took her in his royal arms and said,
In words breathed out in whispers sweet, 'My love.'
To which he read reply in loving eyes   440
Of this sweet child, who too, alas! drank deep
Of pleasure's cup just for a fleeting hour,
Whose taste is spoiled by bitter dregs anon.

V

It was not long when news was blazed abroad
About Thuthula's flight from Gaxa's home.
The royal beads rolled up in mat were found,
Her whereabouts her father did not know.
The Xhosas, hunters born, did trace her step
Across the Fish up to the Tyume bounds.
Then with abhorring hands they said: 'The chief
Has done great ill this woman to abduct.'
And Mguye, Ngqika's counsellor, was blamed
As prime among King Ngqika's trusted men.
Out of the west a threatening cloud did rise.
It grew in size, in colour too more dark,
And it was plain a thunderstorm was near.
Qamata's wrath—transgression of the law
And custom did bring. So it must be.

God works through man His purpose to achieve.
The Ndlambe tribe in counsel did consult.   460
The messengers of war from royal kraal
Took news to all the sub-chiefs of the tribe.
A day was named for impis to report.
The warriors sharpened *izikempe* spears,
Ijozi too and ox-hide shields were tried.
The women ground *utshongo*, food for war,
And then the hordes held muster at great place.
They came in bands, each as a regiment,
According to their clans. The chieftains led.
Soon all have come, there sounds the war song grave.
There stands the chief, the army to address.

'Thuthula's gone, the woman of the tribe.
Her track is said to cross the River Fish.
As you all know, no ill was done by me;
My fault was only to bring up a child,
Behold this child has stabbed me in the back.
All you who gather here, I send you on.
I say prevent this branch from hitting me,
I do not know the cause; the same with you.
Look there he is, ye sons of Phalo great,   480
Ye sons of Tshwo bold and Ngconde brave.'

With feeling spake Rarabe's son that day.
Imbongi too a string of praises sang
As he did strut around the royal folds.
Itola too his rites mysterious made
And in the river all the army washed.
Then like a mamba black the swarm uncoiled.
They go to fight to win the beauty home,
To right the wrong against the Ndlambe tribe.

Among the Ngqika tribe, danger was sensed,
The women gave alarm that war was nigh.
To royal place the impis summoned were.

Although a man some enemies may have,
His friends again are numbered by their tens.
Among Chief Ngqika's councillors 'twas so.
A number knew quite nothing of this plan
Of dark conspiracy which caused the fire.
These did support most loyally their chief.
The Ndlambes too knew nothing of this plan
Of base conspiracy with motive strange.   500
One thing they knew, Thuthula stolen was.
The Ngqikas all had done this shameful deed.
They burned the huts and left no kraal untouched.
Destroying, plundering, they drove the spoil,
And like a forest fire they left a waste,
Until one day they face to face did meet
These armies of related chiefs by birth,
On that great plain, the bloody plain of death,
A swarm of dusky forms in multitudes.
The spears against the sun did dazzle eye.
The shield was man's sole hiding-place that day.
The vanguards of the armies led the hosts,
The scouts behind in Xhosa fashion true,
Intshinga and iQauka army main.
The flanks were held by the *inkongo* swift.
Uqoqo braves the rearguard did compose.
The men of royal blood were there that day
And heroes brave, the *izithwala-ndwe*.
They stood not sizing up each other long.
A man was heard to say, 'Tsi ha! the arms   520

Of Chief Rarabe.' Slaughter red began.
The *indwe* man another *indwe* met,
The common man another commoner.
'Right into battle,' urged the voice of man,
With fury slaying right and left with might.
The spear did stab, and reeked in man's heart blood,
For fierce the battle which that morn was fought.
The day wore on, the wounded lay in heaps,
And when the sun did seek the western hills
The Ngqika wall collapsed, the brave were done.
They beat retreat; defeated remnants fled.
Courageous Umrotshozo heroes fell
For these Chief Ngqika shed some bitter tears,
His braves, the bodyguard, the trusted men,
The comrades, friends and mates he loved so well,
They were propitiation for the wrong—
The sin—outcome of dark conspiracy.
That day were found some widows in the tribe,
And orphans too. Thuthula was the cause.

Ntsikana and Chief Ngqika did escape.   540
In course of time the kindlers of the fire
Were found out, and their motives too divulged.
But they had paid the price of sin full well
With blood of life on battlefield that day.
Their bodies were the food of vultures wild.
Thuthula was returned to Ndlambe's kraal
And she was pardoned for her lapse, because
She had been made unwittingly a bait
To trap Ntsikana and Chief Ngqika, thus
To banish this the Gospel of the Lord.
Henceforth, however, was Lwaganda weaned

From Word of God. His people were appeased.
But often he was heard to sigh with grief,
And pained at heart, he would confess and say,
'Had I a friend, he would report my state
In heaven.' A heavenly vision never dies,
Take note from Mlawu's son, Chief Ngqika great.

Today all these our actors are no more.
Chief Ngqika—Xhosa king—himself is dead.
Gone is the seer Ntsikana—Gaba's son.   560
But this great Truth continues still to live.
It sought itself some other followers.
Those days the sun was rising in the east;
Today, rejoice, the sun has left the hills.

(Abridged)

Notes on the Poems

A TALE OF THE MAIZE PLANT, *page* 9.

12. *olugbere rats:* rats used as ingredients in the medicinal charms which confer the power to utter effective curses.

13. *fishes of the olugbala breed:* fish used as ingredients in the medicinal charms which ensure a safe escape in accidents.

14. *kola nuts:* the fruit of the kola tree. In West Africa they are offered to visitors as a sign of friendship.

37. *Yorubas:* a people who predominate in Western Nigeria.

38. *Fulanis:* a nomadic people who, since the fourteenth century, have spread over West Africa. In the nineteenth century they created a number of powerful kingdoms.

58. *B'o-jogun-erin-a-gba-a-l''o-re:* 'If he gained a horse from a legacy, it would be taken from him.'

87. *Elerineye Omo'le Jagun:* 'Having laughter of dignity, son of the house of Jagun.'

THE TROUBLE-LOVER, *page* 12.

19. *The Iron God:* Ogun, the Yoruba god of war and iron.

23. *We owe the neighbours sympathetic greetings oft:* 'There will be many occasions on which we have to express our sympathy to the neighbours in their suffering.'

33. *Shango:* the Yoruba god of thunder and lightning.

37. *mortar:* the bowl made from the trunk of a tree in which the women pound grain—maize, millet, yam, according to locality. In this poem it is personified.

39. *yam:* the tuber of a tropical plant. It is the staple diet of the people in many parts of West Africa.

40. *Oba:* the title of a Yoruba chief.

ANCESTRAL FACES, *page* 15.

1. *limbo:* the condition of being neglected or forgotten. The poem speaks of the dead, unable to free themselves from the pursuits of life, returning to find the living also are unchanged.

9. *cowries:* small shells formerly used as money in West Africa.

YOU MAY WELL CRY, *page* 16.

A speech from the close of John Pepper Clark's play, *The Song of a Goat.* It is a comment on the deaths of the main characters which have just occurred, and on the difficulty of understanding the meaning of the tragedy.

7. *for laugh:* 'for laughter.'

NIGHT RAIN, *page* 17.

10. *Droning with insistent ardour upon . . ..* Rain is falling upon the roof, and the water is coming in through the sheaves of the thatch which are thin enough for the flashes of lightning to be seen through them. The water drips past the roof rafters underneath, which it is too dark for the poet to see clearly.

19. *Much like beads I could in prayer tell:* The drops of water falling into the bowls set to catch them could be used by the poet like the beads of a rosary, for counting his prayers

37. *iroko tree:* African teak.

IBADAN, *page* 18.

Ibadan is the capital of Western Nigeria. Its rusting corrugated iron roofs cover many square miles.

REINCARNATION, *page* 19.

The spirits of the dead return in the form of waves falling on the shore at night and through the sound of human breath and of the wind. At morning the poet turns away from them to the dawn.

THE LINES OF OUR HANDS, *page* 20.
5. *homeric fights:* battles between great heroes such as are described in the poetry of the ancient Greek poet Homer.

VIATICUM, *page* 23.
'Viaticum' originally meant the preparations and provisions for a journey (here, the journey of life). In the Catholic Church it is the name for the Communion given to a person in danger of death as preparation for the journey to the next life. The poet uses this word with strong Christian associations as the title of a poem about a traditional African ceremony which assures him the protective presence of his ancestors throughout his life.

BREATH, *page* 25.
47–49. . . . *our fate is bound to the law,*
  And the fate of the dead who are not dead
  To the spirits of breath who are stronger than they.
The life of man is bound to the life of nature because nature is full of the spirits of the human dead, and these in turn are bound to what the poet calls the Spirits of Breath, the spirit of nature itself.

WAVES, *page* 27.
5. *All those poisoned with fatal creeds:* all those in the grip of fatalistic beliefs which make it impossible for them to conceive how their situation can ever be changed for the better.

TIMES, *page* 28.

'To everything there is a season, and a time to every purpose under the heaven'; but we do not live only in the present. Living today we create the future and the future (the poet is thinking particularly of the political freedom and stability he hopes for) is present as a seed even in the troubled present.

BIRD'S EYE-VIEW, *page* 33.

The poet, a young Nigerian student, going to study in England, describes the experience through the imagery of the English winter and of a bird that has lost its freedom.

5. *handed darkness early:* in winter, darkness falls much earlier in England than anywhere in Africa.

THE GHOSTS, *page* 36.

23–42. These lines refer to the violence and terror that followed the formation of the Ashanti National Liberation Movement in Kumasi in late 1954, in opposition to Dr Nkrumah's government.

98. *Twedeampong:* 'Nyame, the Ashanti Supreme Being or sky god.

THE MEANING OF AFRICA, *page* 42.

The poet describes his feelings on returning to Africa after a long period during which he lived in England and took part there in the movement for African independence by addressing meetings and broadcasting. He considers the real Africa he finds against the image he has held in his mind during his absence.

9. *a vision euphemistic:* a vision which overlooks the unpleasant parts of reality.

46. *go for bush:* West African pidgin English for: Go into the bush, or remote countryside.

76. *his motto painted on:* in West Africa, the lorries used as buses usually have a motto or a text painted on them.

WERE I TO CHOOSE, *page* 46.
A poem written in a style owing much to that of the Welsh poet Dylan Thomas. The poet considers how he was conceived in the womb, how his crying as a new-born child stands for the griefs of his future years. Now, at thirty-one years, his thoughts are confused and only death brings calm. Neither to be born nor to die is in our choice.
21. *harmattan:* a hot, dry wind in West Africa that blows from the Sahara Desert from December to February.

FOR GEORGETTE, *page* 48.
3. *the newcomer:* a new-born child.

APOCALYPSE, *page* 50.
3. *turn to blood the moon:* Joel, Ch. 2, v. 31.
12. *miracle of spears and pruning hooks:* Isaiah, Ch. 2, v. 4.
17. *Sasabonsam:* a hairy monster, with long legs and feet pointing both ways, that lives in the heart of the forest and is hostile to men.

CACTUS, *page* 55.
16. *Iarivo:* another name for Antananarivo, capital of the Merina Kings and Queens of the High Plateau since the early nineteenth century, and capital of modern Madagascar.

THREE DAYBREAKS, *page* 57.
21. *sleeper in the ocean:* the sun.
29. *lapidist:* a lapidary or cutter and polisher of precious stones. He uses his mills to grind the faces of the stone.

The poet represents Night preparing a precious stone, which is the dawn.

SPIDER, *page* 59.

18. *turns the spider's ambush:* goes round it and so causes the ambush to fail.

TWO OLD MERINA SONGS, *page* 60.

The Merina tribe made its home on the High Plateau of Madagascar and was to a large extent responsible for the unification of Madagascar in the nineteenth century, before the French annexation.

1. *two stones:* two lovers.

BLUE, BLUE, THE EYE OF HEAVEN, *page* 61.

The author was arrested after the 1947 uprising against French rule in Madagascar, and he wrote this poem while in prison. In style, it resembles some of the poetry of the nineteenth-century French poet, Paul Verlaine.

POPULAR LOVE-SONG, *page* 63.

1. *my cousin:* in traditional Malagasy love-poetry, lovers refer to one another as cousins (cf. p. 60, l. 59).

28. *valiha:* Malagasy musical instrument made of bamboo and similar to the guitar.

CHOICE, *page* 65.

12. *rice water:* a drink made from rice, the staple food of Madagascar.

ZEBU, *page* 65.

The Zebu or humped ox is very common in Madagascar.

TRADITIONAL THEME FROM MERINA, *page 66.*

23. *avoko:* an edible plant.
24. *papango:* kite, bird of prey of the falcon family.
60. *zozoro reeds:* a papyrus-like reed found in Madagascar.

STANLEY MEETS MUTESA, *page 68.*

Henry Morton Stanley (1841–1904) was an American journalist and explorer. Mutesa was the Kabaka or King of Buganda who received Stanley with great pomp and hospitality in 1875. Stanley gives a description of the occasion in his Diaries.

22. *Masai:* a warlike tribe that has its home in Kenya.
29. *Nyanza:* a large lake in East Africa.

ALL DAY LONG, *page 72.*

3. *Cayor, Baol:* provinces of Senegal.
7. *Sine:* province of Senegal from which Senghor comes.

NDESSÉ, *page 73.*

Ndessé is a Serer word meaning blues, sadness.

2. *gymnic feast:* a reference to the wrestling matches held among the Serers of Senegal.
4. *Kor-Sanou!:* exclamation meaning: 'champion of Sanou.'
4. *Katamague:* the coast to the south of Dakar where Senghor was born.
10. *As when good Serer women . . .:* Senghor writes in one of his essays: 'I remember my Serer grandmothers used to have recourse to God in times of great distress. They would dress like men, with all the trappings, fire guns and shoot arrows into the air. They would even go so far as to use vulgar language in French.'
11. *paragnessé:* a popular Serer corruption of the word *français,* French.
15. *marabout:* Muslim religious teacher. It is customary in

West Africa for parents to give their children into his care for their religious education. These are the disciples referred to.

TAGA FOR MBAYE DYOB, *page* 74.
taga: lament.
tama: a small drum used by *griots* (West African troubadours), carried under the arm.
11. *Rivers of the South:* the rivers of Casamance, a very picturesque region in Southern Senegal.
16. *griot:* pronounced *gree-o*. In Senegal, troubadour poets and actors, once retained by noble families to sing their praises and genealogies; they enjoyed the right to criticize freely.
22. *from Ngabu to the Walo, from Ngalam to the sea:* Ngabu and Ngalam are far inland in Senegal, and the Walo is the name of a region on the banks of the Senegal River near the coast. The poet emphasizes that the songs of the young girls will be heard throughout the country.
23. *kora:* a type of harp in Senegal.

MESSAGE, *page* 77.
9. *the tribes that let fly a poisonous greeting:* i.e. who shoot poisonous arrows or darts at strangers.
13. *kailcedrat:* a shady tree found in Senegal.
15. *Elissa:* place in northern Portuguese Guinea from which Senghor's family originally came.
22. *you decline the rose:* a reference to the learning of Latin, where *rosa* is used in grammar books as the model for the first declension.
22. *your ancestors the Gauls:* a French history text-book, formerly used in primary schools in French West Africa, began with a reference to *our ancestors the Gauls*.
23. *Sorbonne:* the name for the Faculties of Arts and Science in the University of Paris.

24. *golden louis:* gold coins of the reign of the French King Louis XIV.

30. *Mbissel, Fa'oy:* two pagan shrines near Senghor's birthplace.

41. *ivory message:* a reference to the carved ivory staff carried by a chief's messenger when he bears a message to another chief.

TELEPHONE CONVERSATION, *page* 81.

An African is looking for accommodation in London where those who let rooms are sometimes unwilling or reluctant to take Africans. In London people of all shades of colour are found and racial prejudice is sometimes stronger against people of darker skin-colour. This comic poem tells of the poet's embarrassment at being asked how dark he is, and how he was able to repay the landlady's rudeness.

11. *Button A. Button B.:* the poet in his embarrassment stares about him, at the telephone controls, at the public telephone box from which he is calling, at a pillar box outside and at a passing bus.

23–24. *spectroscopic flight of fancy:* consideration or analysis in the mind of different shades of colour.

A BUS RIDE, *page* 82.

18. *abi na wetin:* an exclamation of impatience in Nigerian pidgin English.

THUTHULA, *page* 83.

Thuthula was the youngest wife of Ndlambe. The poem tells the story of her abduction by her husband's nephew, the Xhosa Paramount Chief Ngqika, who lived from 1775 to 1828. He had been left Paramount Chief of the Rarabe branch of the Xhosa people while still a child. Ndlambe, his father's brother, had been made regent and was able to keep Ngqika from taking power into his hands until 1818. Relations between the two men were strained and when Nqgika abducted his uncle's wife, war broke out. The Xhosa people regarded Ngqika's action as incestuous and most of the clans turned against him. A fierce and bloody battle was fought at Amalinde in 1818 where Ngqika's army was routed with great loss of life. This is the battle described in the poem. Ngqika sought the aid of the British and a year later Ndlambe was defeated. At this period Christianity was beginning to make progress among the Xhosa people and Jolobe sees the abduction of Thuthula as a plot to halt the spread of Christianity. Historically the religious issue was probably not so important.

4. *Chief Phalo:* a great Chief of the Xhosa (1700–75). He had two sons: Galeka (his heir) and Rarabe, the right-hand son.

5. *the right-hand sons:* these are the sons of the Chief's second wife. The eldest son of the Chief's first wife, i.e. the son of the Great or Royal House, is heir to the Chieftainship. The eldest of the right-hand sons usually formed a new clan within the tribe.

6. *illustrious chief Rarabe:* Rarabe (1722–87) was the eldest son of Phalo's right-hand wife. A disagreement arose between him and the heir, Galeka (1730–92), and he afterwards formed a separate branch of the Xhosa tribe— the Ama-Rarabe.

10. *they bred the racing oxen for their sport . . . :* ox-racing was a very popular sport among the Xhosa.

15. *Gaxa's home:* Gaxa was the name of Ndlambe's racing ox, and so his kraal becomes known as 'Gaxa's home'.

39. *Qamata:* God.

50. *she saw a greyhound cross . . .:* the Xhosa had acquired greyhounds from the Europeans and used them as hunting dogs.

57. *Chief Mlawu's son, the prince:* Ngqika, grandson of Rarabe. Mlawu actually died before his father, so had never ruled as Chief of the Xhosa.

59. *his paternal uncle:* Ndlambe, Mlawu's brother by the same mother.

100. *the Ma-Xhosa tribe: Ama* (or as here *Ma*) is a Xhosa plural prefix. The Xhosa tribe settled in the Eastern Cape Province in the seventeenth century. After the death of Chief Phalo, they split into two sections, one under Galeka, son of 'the great house', the other under Rarabe, the 'right-hand son'.

137. *Yese's party:* Yese was Ngqika's mother. The mother of the Paramount Chief had great power, so Yese would naturally be anxious for her son effectively to assume the Chieftainship, especially as it became more and more obvious that Ndlambe was reluctant to relinquish the Regency.

138–39. *. . . the day Chief Khawuta came,*
        And placed around his neck the royal beads.
Khawuta (1760–1820), Paramount Chief of the Galeka branch of the Xhosa tribe, came to officiate at Ngqika's public installation as Paramount Chief of the Rarabe branch. This he did by placing around his neck the red beads that are the Chief's insignia.

142. *Lwaganda:* the name by which Ngqika was known at his court.

143. *The Tshulubembe great, etc.:* the people sing the praises of the new Chief in traditional fashion. The Xhosa praise songs are in rich, metaphorical and often archaic language.

147. *Nkwebus:* a Xhosa clan mixed with Hottentot blood.

The Hottentots were a light-skinned people already living in the Cape area when the Xhosa people arrived.

152. *Amaphakathi:* the counsellors of the Chief. The Xhosa Chiefs have a court of counsellors whose advice they are bound to take.

152. *Chief Ndlambe proud:* Ngqika's uncle, the Regent. This and the lines that follow show Ndlambe's ambitions.

167. *lobola:* cattle given by a man to the parents of his future wife.

174. *A spear, betrothal's sign, was left in court:* a man wishing to marry a young woman will leave a spear at her home, taking care that he is seen. If the spear is not returned he is acceptable.

182. *The master of the ceremonies:* if the suitor is acceptable, he appoints a 'master of the ceremonies' to negotiate the *lobola* and to make arrangements for the wedding.

184. a royal *khazi: khazi* is the name given to the *lobola* cattle themselves.

191. *By night on my bed, etc.:* from the *Song of Solomon*, Ch. 3, vv. 1–2.

200–201. *There were mpothulo and inqhakhwe cows,*
And also famous ubulunga beast.

The bride goes in procession to the bridegroom's home, taking with her three cows. The first, the *mpothulo* cow, is used to feed the bridal party until the wedding is over. The second, the *inqhakhwe* cow, provides the bride with milk and is a symbol of her independence. The third, the *ubulunga* cow, is a sacred cow, of which the wife is sole possessor. It may not be taken from her by her husband for any reason whatsoever. The bride makes a necklace out of the hairs of its tail to protect her and her children from misfortune.

202. *ingqongqo drum:* a drum made of ox-skin played by the women during the wedding dance.

205. *umdudo:* the first movement of the wedding dance, performed by the older men. They line up in rows and stamp the ground with their feet in unison.

206. *the active ngqaqhu step:* the second movement of the wedding dance, which, because it requires great agility and stamina, is always performed by the younger men.

208. *The last step* umtyhulubo, *now does sound,*
    Men quiver here like reeds on river bank.
    The third and last movement of the wedding dance, in which the upper part of the body is made to quiver vigorously.

225. *Ntsikana:* a convert to Christianity who tried to persuade the Ngqikas to avoid war with Ndlambe which he foresaw would be disastrous.

227. *Hulushe:* the name of Ntsikana's racing ox.

231. *van der Kemp:* a missionary of the London Missionary Society who worked among the Hottentots of South Africa in the early part of the nineteenth century. Christian influence among the Xhosa at this time came mainly from his mission.

235. *inqhina* band: a hunting party.

243. *Nokhonongo:* Ntsikana's court name.

257. *Forthwith he cleansed himself of ochre red:* the Xhosa smear themselves with red clay on festive occasions.

264. *Jwara:* the clan name of the Sogas. Jothelo Soga was a famous Xhosa warrior and counsellor.

280. *I-Ntab'eGqira and the Hogsback mount:* names of mountains.

360. *kraal:* the complex of huts used by one family.

433. *Ntlebi:* one of Ngqika's counsellors.

460. *The Ndlambe tribe:* it was customary among the Xhosa for the tribe to take its name from the reigning Chief. The poet talks further on of the Ngqika tribe.

463. *impi:* Xhosa regiment.

464. *izikempe spears:* short stabbing spear with a broad blade, for use at close quarters.

465. *ijozi spears:* a stabbing spear with a broad blade, but longer shaft than the *izikempe* spears.

466. *utshongo:* ground, roasted maize.

469. *According to their clans . . .:* the Xhosa army consisted of regiments made up of clans under the chief of the clan.

471. *There stands the chief, the army to address :* the chief is, of course, Ndlambe. It was customary for the chief to address his army before battle, and the lines that follow are almost exactly the speech Ndlambe made on this occasion, as preserved in Xhosa oral tradition.

481. *Tshiwo:* Chief Phalo's father (died about 1702).

481. *Ngconde:* Chief Tshiwo's father.

483. *Imbongi:* the court poet who sang the praises of the Chief whom he accompanied everywhere. He is similar perhaps to the *griots* of West Africa.

485. *Itola:* the war-doctor, who was charged with preparing the warriors to face battle.

512–16. *The vanguards of the armies . . .:* an accurate description of the usual Xhosa battle formation.

514. *Intshinga:* section of the army composed of royal clans.

514. *iQauka:* section of the army composed of commoners.

515. *inkongo:* the flying column of the army.

516. *uqoqo braves:* the reserve regiment.

518. *the izithwala-ndwe:* the veteran soldiers, honoured for their courage.

522. *ndwe:* another form of *izithwala-ndwe.*

524. *'Right into battle,':* the command to engage at close quarters, with the stabbing spears. It shows the fierceness of the battle.

532. *Umrotshozo:* the name of Ngqika's regiment.

Index of Titles and First Lines